THE CORNBREAD BIBLE

A Recipe Storybook

by
Jennifer Shambrook, Ph.D

All rights reserved © 2012 Jennifer Shambrook

Keywords: cornbread, southern cooking, gluten-free, hushpuppies, homestead, food storage, cookbooks, frugal living, soul food, corn bread, story telling

The Cornbread Bible: A Recipe Storybook

The Cornbread Bible: A Recipe Storybook
Jennifer Shambrook, Ph.D.

Table of Contents

FOREWORD 4
INTRODUCTION TO THE CORNBREAD BIBLE 5
    Recipe Navigation 6
    Cornbread Doctrine 8
    The Care and Feeding of Cast Iron Cookware 9
    Cornmeal snobbery 10
    Is Jiffy Mix 'of the devil?' 10
    Gluten freedom 11
BREADS, MUFFINS AND STICKS, OH MY! 12
    Mama's Easy (Regular Unleaded) Cornbread 13
    The World's Greatest Corn Muffins from Jeannie Martin, WGC 13
    My Sweet Nicole's Sweet Cornbread 14
    Creel's "Must Have" Traditional Cornbread 15
    Granny Tom's Patted Cornpone 16
CORNBREAD WITH STUFF IN IT 20
    Mammaw's Little Baby Loves Crackling Bread 20
    Jalapeno cornbread 22
    Mexican Chili and Chihuahua Muffins 24
    HB's Broccoli Cornbread 26
    Tracy McLean's Chunky Muffins 28
    Tisha's Fancy French Cornbread 30
HUSHPUPPY HEAVEN 32
GRIDDLE CAKES 37
    Uncle Lonnie's Johnnies 37

Frances's Mexican Hot Water Cornbread 38

Juanny Cakes Benedict for Two 38

SIDES AND SUCH 40

Turnip Greens with Cornbread Dumplings 41

Robert's Hot Pepper Sauce for Greens 45

Aunt Pat's New Potatoes with Cornmeal Butter sauce 46

Granny's Squash Casserole 47

Sue Ann's Cornbread Salad 51

DRESSING OR STUFFING 54

My Own Chicken'n'Dressing Recipe 57

Constructing Your Own Pan'o'Dressing Masterpiece 59

MAIN DISHES 64

Cowboys, Cronkite and Cornburger Pie 64

Beanie-Weenie Casserole 68

Butterbean Pie 68

Cornbread Meatloaf 70

Pot Roast Pie 71

Corndogs 72

LAST WORD 76

ABOUT THE AUTHOR 76

FOREWORD

I have had the good fortune to grow up around story-tellers. Both sides of my family love to tell stories. The stories may be to amaze, excite, persuade, inform, or just pass the time of day. As a kid, it was my job to be the audience, to laugh at the funny parts and be a sponge so that I could pass the stories on down. I would listen for hours to my grandparents, uncles, aunts, parents, and cousins.

It was expected that I would get married, raise kids, keep house, and pass the stories down to the next generation or two. That's what everyone expected, even me. Little did I know that my path would take some unusual turns that would eventually lead to a Ph.D. in Public Health with a focus on occupational stress. Those early lessons in story telling are what helped me to learn to be inquisitive, and listen, and be a sponge, and then ask my own questions and tell my own stories in the academic realm.

I learned that I loved to write academic papers. Papers with statistics and comparisons and graphs and charts and questions and data and conclusions are fun for me. So much so that I've won some awards and eventually became the editor of a peer reviewed academic journal. I've been blessed and I've worked hard. My parents and extended family were good examples of that.

Even in my fifties, I still love for my parents to be proud of me and "brag on me" to their friends. They are impressed that I have papers published. They are proud of me even though the papers look like complete gibberish and win awards that no one they know has ever heard of and I get invited to nerd-fests all over the world to talk about the gibberish and accept the awards.

No matter where I go, what I do, or what I learn, I'm still the girl who grew up eating cornbread, barefooted, in Hebron Valley. I still love to cook and have a garden and home can food for my family. I still love to hear all those family stories… and now be one of the storytellers to the next generation of inquisitive little sponges. This book includes some of those stories that just pass the time of day and give a glimpse of years gone by.

I wrote this book because I wanted to write something that my family and friends might actually enjoy reading and find useful in some way. I wanted to write something for and about the people I love. There are notes sections tucked in here and there so you can personalize the book with your own favorite memories and memorable favorites.

So, here it is for all my family and all my friends and for all the world that might be interested in:

The Cornbread Bible: A Recipe Storybook.

INTRODUCTION TO THE CORNBREAD BIBLE

I hope you and whoever you feed are all going to LOVE what you learn as you read this book!

Cornbread is a staple in Southern cooking. When I was growing up in the Appalachian foothills of Alabama, it was inconceivable that we would ever sit down to the supper table without a steaming hot plate of cornbread being a part of the meal. As a matter of fact, the main meal of the day was usually timed to when the cornbread finished cooking so the cornbread could be served piping hot with a mouthwatering steam rising from it. The delicious taste and smell of hot buttered cornbread is pure heaven to experience. What many do not realize is how very EASY cornbread is to make!

The Cornbread Bible will serve as your ready reference to your old favorites or new experiences with one of the absolute EASIEST, most economical, versatile and tastiest breads on the planet: Cornbread! We are going to look at traditional cornbread in its many variations, cornbread with stuff in it, cornbread sides, main dishes with cornbread toppings, corndogs, and the queen of all cornbread concoctions: cornbread dressing (you may know it as stuffing.)

As you can see, there is so much more to cornbread than cornbread alone. There is also more to The Cornbread Bible than food. When my family gets together to eat, we don't just eat the food, we talk about it. So, I'm not just going to give you recipes, I want to share a few stories to go along with it. Some of my family and friends may have already heard the stories, but that's okay. As my Daddy always likes to say: "If you've already heard this story, don't stop me, I want to hear it again myself!"

Cornbread is quick. Cornbread is easy. Cornbread is delicious. Cornbread is versatile. And, if prepared without the addition of wheat flour, cornbread is naturally gluten-free. Some of these recipes are already gluten free, others can be if you substitute your favorite alternative flour or substitute unleavened cornmeal and baking powder for self-rising cornmeal mix.

Of course, the first thing that comes to mind when daydreaming about cornbread is a piping hot slab of cornbread slathered in butter. The mouth-watering aroma rises with the steam as the butter melts into the bread. Ahhh, let's just take a moment of silence here to enjoy that mental image, shall we? Mmmmmmmmmmmmm.

But as wonderful as that mental image may be, what I imagine and what you imagine may not be the same thing. Cornbread comes in a lot of different varieties. Just in my own immediate family we have had several variations. My mother made a moist cornbread with eggs and sweet milk. Her mother, Granny Tom, made patted corn pone that was rather coarse and crumbly made with stone ground cornmeal, baking soda, buttermilk and no eggs. Both Granny Tom and Mama baked in cast iron and broke their bread into serving pieces rather than cutting with a knife.

My daddy's mother, Mammaw, made sweet cornbread with milk, lots of eggs, and sugar. She baked her bread in a sheet cake pan and cut it into about twenty squares because she was often cooking for a houseful. A pan of cornbread, a pot of beans on the stove, and some sliced onions in the fridge, would feed a meal to anyone that happened to drop by. If you dropped by, she always wanted you "sit a spell" and eat "a little something" before you left.

Mammaw was also either humble enough or bold enough (I'm not sure which) to bust out a box of Jiffy Mix® to make a quick pan of cornbread if the crowd was smallish and time was shortish and she was tiredish when the cornbread craving hit. Other kinfolk would make cornsticks or corn muffins or triangle shaped cornbread pieces that were baked in a cast iron pan divided into wedges.

Many people have very strong preferences for one type of cornbread over another. Some will even actually refuse to eat cornbread that isn't of their particular cornbread genre. As for me, I like all kinds of cornbread. My preference, when at a potluck dinner and given a choice of more than one kind of cornbread, will be determined by what I am going to eat with the cornbread. No matter what, if cornbread is available when I'm fixing my plate, you'll most assuredly find a piece of cornbread on said plate when I sit down to partake.

In addition to different variations of cornbread, we are also going to visit hushpuppy heaven, griddle cakes (which go by many different names), side dishes, main dishes, and an all-time favorite at my house: corndogs. And I am talking about the absolutely BEST corndogs you have ever put in your mouth! As a bonus to those who have proclaimed their gluten freedom, these corndogs are gluten free!

Recipe Navigation

The Cornbread Bible recipes are divided into several sections. We will start with oven baked cornbreads, muffins and sticks. In that section you'll find recipes for traditional and sweet cornbread, corn pone with instructions on how to eat it with butter and molasses, crackling bread, and the world's greatest corn muffins. There are also recipes for Broccoli Cornbread, Jalapeno Cornbread, and a game-day favorite called Chihuahua Muffins… and more!

There is a special section devoted to my own personal favorite form of cornbread: hushpuppies. From there we move on to the cornbread/hushpuppy hybrid that is cooked on a griddle and called by various names such as Johnny Cake, Journey Cake, or hot water cornbread.

My long-time dear friend, Nancy Whitcroft, has recently had to proclaim her gluten freedom. She really missed one of our favorites: Corndogs. I have developed and included a great recipe for some really scrumptious corndogs, so we have a section dedicated to that wonderful taste sensation.

From top left to right: Mixed greens with cornbread dumplings, Chili Muffins, Jalapeno Cornbread, and Chihuahua Muffins

You will find a chapter on side dishes with cornbread elements, such as mixed greens with cornbread dumplings and squash casserole.

There is also a chapter on main dishes like chicken'n'dressing and cornbread topped butterbean pie which is a great one-dish meal. Also included is my Mama's Cornburger Pie, which was one of my very favorite dishes when I was growing up.

As I said earlier, there are stories sprinkled all along the way. I am not really sure if this is a recipe book with stories or a story book with recipes, but either way, I hope you'll enjoy them all!

This picture is from my *Great Cornbread Cookathon* where I cooked four different recipes in one night. All of the recipes in the Cornbread Bible have been tested to insure that the measurements, ingredients and cooking times are right.

Many long-time cornbread cooks don't really use measurements as much as we cook by our senses. Does that batter look thick enough? Does that bread smell like it's ready to come out of the oven? Does this hushpuppy taste onion-y enough? Did you hear the batter sizzle when you poured it into the skillet? If you are an old hand at cornbread cookery, you know exactly what I mean.

If this is a new domestic art form for you, then you will learn the basic principles very quickly and soon be fine-tuning your own variations of these recipes. In the Dressing/Stuffing section, you will learn to develop your own signature recipe using some simple, basic principles and your own creative genius.

Cornbread Doctrine

Believe it or not, some people have VERY STRONG FEELINGS about what a properly made pan of cornbread should be. I have personally witnessed extreme family discord (fortunately not in my own family) ensue over just this issue. It has been said by a multitude of cornbread purists of my own close acquaintance that sweet cornbread does not qualify as *true* or *real* cornbread. I have even witnessed rude angry outbursts related to this very subject when someone unknowingly bit into a piece of sweet cornbread without being forewarned.

On the other hand, I have known those who prefer sweet cornbread leave a perfectly good slab of traditional cornbread on their plate to be tossed out with the trash with only one bite having been consumed. This should never be. That orphaned cornbread could have gone unmolested into the freezer for the next pan of chicken'n'dressing.

Please don't get me wrong. I'm not saying that you should save a piece of cornbread that someone has man-handled, taken a bite out of, found unsatisfactory to their personal cornbread requirements, then left tainted and pitifully rejected on their plate. What I am proposing is that we post a suitable warning that the cornbread is or is not of *varietus cornbreadius sweetimus*. This way, folks can make their decision of whether or not they are going to eat it **before** they plop said cornbread slab on their plates. What I am promoting here is some sort of early detection warning system here for the prevention of cornbread waste and abuse due to sweetness level. Petition to Congress to follow sometime in the future.

Each to their own… cornbread preference is personal. One of my goals in putting together the Cornbread Bible is to provide an equal opportunity recipe storybook that will have many recipes you will enjoy whatever your preference may be. It is also my goal to teach the basic principles of cornbread construction so that you feel confident in making the slight adjustments that make your own recipes unique and precisely to your own tastes. Feel free to tweak these recipes with wild abandon. Make them your own.

The Care and Feeding of Cast Iron Cookware

With each recipe, a recommended cooking vessel may be suggested by the recipe creator. Many times, it will be some form of cast iron. Do you absolutely have to have a cast iron skillet to make cornbread? Well, no, not really. But for the best and most authentic flavor and texture, using cast iron is going to get you there. Will it still be delicious and good even if you cook in a different pan? Of course it will… just not AS good in my humble opinion. It will make a difference, but not a deal-breaker.

You can find cast iron skillets, griddles, divided cornbread wedge pans, corn stick pans (shown here), and even cast iron muffin pans at www.amazon.com, Wal-Mart, Bass Pro Shoppes, and Target stores. They are very reasonably priced, usually in the $20 neighborhood, and most come pre-seasoned and ready to use right out of the box. I recommend those from Lodge ironworks as they are pre-seasoned.

If your iron pan is not pre-seasoned, seasoning cast iron is a fairly easy process to go through. My cousin Katie recommended that I be sure to tell my readers how to season and care for cast iron. So, say thank you to Katie DeShazo Antonio if this was just what you needed to know.

Seasoning a Cast Iron Skillet

It's a fairly easy process. Start preheating your oven at 350*F. While the oven is heating, take a thickness of about 3 paper towels folded into quarters to make a pad. Pour about a tablespoon of vegetable oil into the skillet or pan. Rub the oil all around the skillet, inside and out, to completely coat. If you run out of oil, just pour in a little more.

Put the cast iron vessel into the oven and allow it to bake for about an hour, then turn the oven off and let it cool completely. You may even allow it to cool overnight. Remove the cooled cast iron from the oven. Wipe down thoroughly with clean paper towels.

Your cast iron will stay seasoned by being used. Each time you cook with cast iron, you add a little oil to the skillet or pan and place it in the oven as the oven preheats. After using the cast iron, just wipe it out with clean paper towels and put it away. It would be very rare for something to stick to your cast iron, or for it to get rusty, if you use it regularly. But there are easy remedies if this does happen.

If the cast iron has something to stick to it, pour in some salt and rub with a paper towel to scour. If necessary, re-season. If the cast iron gets rusty, scrub with steel wool and a little vegetable oil. Wipe out with a damp cloth and re-season.

We have cast iron skillets in our family that has been handed down for generations. It is durable, beautiful, fairly inexpensive, low maintenance and yields the best cornbread the world has ever known! Viva la cast iron!

Cornmeal snobbery

I try not to be a cornmeal snob, but do sympathize with said snobbery in others. I usually use self-rising cornmeal mix in my own cornmeal endeavors. I am more frugal than particular when it comes to cornmeal brand. If they have self-rising cornmeal mix at Aldi's, I get it there for cheap. If not, I buy whatever is the best buy at another store. I like Cabin Home, Martha White, Aunt Jemimah, White Lily or whatever I can find. My favorite is the kind that has buttermilk flavoring in it.

Some people have strong preferences for a particular cornmeal, as you will see when you are reading through some of the cornbread stories. Some prefer white over yellow, or yellow over white. Some prefer coarse grind over fine grind. I only have a strong preference for self-rising mix over plain with a definite tilt toward white over yellow.

Lest I be guilty of deception of my dear readers, I must confess that I do have one tiny inclination toward cornmeal snobbery. When I was living up north I soon found myself smuggling self-rising cornmeal into the Commonwealth of Pennsylvania. I just found it very hard to adapt to the very finely ground unleavened yellow cornmeal with a Quaker on a round oatmeal-looking box. There was just something that smacked of the ridiculous about that.

Don't get me wrong, nothing at all against Quakers, one of my very best friends is a Quaker. But honestly, they have no business showing up on my cornmeal. Furthermore, cornmeal has absolutely no business residing in an oatmeal box. Some things just should not be. I can forgive sugar in cornbread, I can even overlook hushpuppies without onions in them, but I do have to draw the line *somewhere!*

You may want to try different kinds of cornmeal to see if you actually have a real or imagined preference. Whatever creates the best cornbread experience for you is what you should use. Fortunately, cornmeal is a very inexpensive item and you can often afford to splurge on the best without putting a gaping hole in your food budget.

Is Jiffy Mix 'of the devil?'

It may seem an extreme contradiction that I would take offense at Quaker-festooned boxes of cornmeal, and then defend Jiffy Mix. Well, there is a time and a place for everything. I *did* use the Quaker clad cornmeal… when that's all you can get, you are mightily grateful for it. But it made me just *feel funny*.

Jiffy Mix is super-mega-ultra easy. It is everything its name implies. Jiffy Mix is an efficiency measure. Purchasing a box of Jiffy Mix is less of a commitment than going whole hog and buying 5 lbs of meal and a carton of buttermilk.

Think of Jiffy Mix is an introductory cornbread instrument. What we have here is Cornbread 101. Symbolically, you gingerly dip your toe into your first experience with cornbread batter with Jiffy Mix to begin to develop your cornbread senses… which are so crucial to good batter development. Cornbread is super-easy in the first place, but this makes it even easier in its sublime petite pre-measured Jiffiness.

When my Mammaw was too tired to make cornbread, but not too tired to eat it, she would use a box of Jiffy Mix. When my daughter, Nicole, who is living in a house with my precious, much beloved, California-raised, sweet-cornbread-eating son-in-law, can go no longer without a pone of her own, she can whip up a little tray of Jiffy Mix muffins to get her through to her next visit home for some *real* cornbread.

You will find a couple of quick recipes in The Cornbread Bible that call for a box of Jiffy Mix in the recipe. Please don't faint or recoil in disgust. Please just embrace the ease of it all. If you are absolutely unwilling to go the Jiffy Mix route, just substitute a cup of self-rising cornmeal mix instead. I've done that when I didn't have Jiffy Mix on hand and it turned out great.

Gluten freedom

One of my motivations for writing this book came from developing a really good gluten-free corndog recipe for my friend, Nancy Whitcroft. Cornmeal is naturally gluten-free, but self-rising cornmeal mix is not. It has a smidge of wheat flour in it. If you are trying to stay completely gluten free, you can make your own self-rising mix in a small batch to accommodate one recipe or a large batch keep on hand for convenient cornbread construction.

You can make one cup of gluten free cornmeal mix by mixing ¾ cup plus 3 tablespoons of plain cornmeal with 1 teaspoon of baking powder, ¼ teaspoon baking soda and ½ teaspoon of salt.

In the next section where we look at traditional cornbread, you will see recipes that are naturally gluten free. These cornbread recipes can be used for any of the muffin or main dish concoctions.

BREADS, MUFFINS AND STICKS, OH MY!

Here's the real deal, folks. You can cook any of the bread recipes as muffins or sticks. You can cook any of the muffin recipes as cornbread. The only thing that changes whether it is a muffin or a stick or a pone of bread is the pan you cook it in. But just keep an eye on it. If you go from a pone of bread to a mini-muffin, it may not take as long to cook. If you go from a muffin to a bread, it might not be completely cooked in the middle if you use the same time.

It is likely that you will eventually be able to tell if the bread is done simply by the wonderful aroma of cooked cornbread. Until then, you can always tell by checking to see if it is turning brown on top and by inserting a toothpick or sharp knife in the middle and seeing if it comes out clean, or if there is wet batter still in the center.

A big batch of Tracy McLean's delicious Chunky Muffin recipe cooked as a pone of bread, heart-shaped mini-muffins, and corn sticks.

Traditional Southern Cornbread Recipes

Of course, as you might suspect from what's already been said, the easiest way to get cornbread quick, fast and in a hurry is to just snatch up a box of Jiffy Mix and follow the directions in the box. But just for grins, let's say you are ready to move past that point in your cornbread engineering adventures so we'll move on to some slightly more labor intensive methods. Again, NONE of these recipes are difficult. All of these recipes are good and will yield different forms of cornbread wonderfulness. I wanted to give a variety so that my dear readers could experiment with them and see what seems best for them. Your individual cornbread preference is just as valid as anyone else's. If anyone tells you anything different from that, just do what we Southerners have done for centuries: Nod your head, smile, and say "Bless your heart." That is Southern for "I love you way too much to argue." It is also Southern for several other things, but let's bless all of our hearts and stay focused on cornbread here.

Mama's Easy (Regular Unleaded) Cornbread

This is how my Mama taught me to make cornbread. It is so easy. Put oil in the skillet. Put the skillet in the oven. Turn the oven on and mix up the batter using six heaping spoonsful of cornmeal mix, an egg, a little oil, and just enough buttermilk until it looks right. The batter will be ready before the oven preheats and skillet warms up.

Mama adds oil to her batter, but I think the little bit of oil in the skillet that absorbs into the bread is enough for me and I don't need even those few extra calories. I've included it in the recipe, but it is optional. You get to decide how you want to make it.

Ingredients

1. 1 cup self-rising cornmeal mix
2. 1 egg
3. 2 Tablespoons vegetable oil, separated
4. ¾ cups buttermilk

Instructions

1. Pour 1 Tablespoon oil in an 8-9 inch cast iron skillet. Roll from side to side to coat skillet
2. Place skillet in oven and preheat oven to 450* F.
3. Put cornmeal, egg, remaining oil (optional), and buttermilk in mixing bowl and whisk with fork until completely mixed.
4. Remove hot skillet from oven and pour batter in hot skillet (you should hear a sizzle)
5. Bake at 450* for 20-25 minutes or until crust is nicely browned.
6. Remove from oven and immediately flip cornbread with fork so that bottom is facing up.

The World's Greatest Corn Muffins from Jeannie Martin, WGC

Jeannie Martin's husband, cartoonist Mark Martin, is always bragging about being married to the world's greatest cook. He even calls her WGC! Everyone that has ever tasted her food tends to agree with Mark, so I can't say that I blame him at all for shouting from the rooftops what a wonderfully talented and creative woman he is sharing his life (and kitchen table) with! I think she may put in the ultimate secret ingredient in her food. She cooks as an expression of love. If you want them to really turn out to be as good as hers, you will have to do the same.

Jeannie adds the following WGC cornbread tip:

"I flip them over as soon as they come out of the oven to keep them crispy."

World's Greatest Corn Muffins

Ingredients

1. 2 cups minus 2 tablespoons self-rising white cornmeal mix
2. 2 tablespoons self rising flour
3. 1/3 cup canola oil
4. 1 egg
5. 1 2/3 cups buttermilk

Instructions

1. Grease a standard muffin tin or cornstick pan with oil, cooking spray, or shortening
2. Place muffin tin in oven and heat oven to 400* F
3. While oven is heating, mix together cornmeal mix and flour.
4. Add oil, egg, and buttermilk to dry ingredients and mix into batter.
5. Remove hot greased muffin tin or cornstick pan from the oven.
6. Pour batter into hot pan, dividing equally between cells.
7. Bake in 400* oven until browned and centers test done with a sharp knife.

My Sweet Nicole's Sweet Cornbread

My daughter married a man raised in California. He doesn't have the same enthusiasm for cornbread that was instilled in an Alabama-raised girl. He does like cornbread, but his preference is for sweet cornbread… so, Nicole has learned to make and appreciate sweet cornbread. Although Erek eats the cornbread with his meal, Nicole puts butter and syrup on hers and just eats it for dessert.

Sweet Cornbread Method

Instructions

1. Put 1 tablespoon of vegetable oil in a 8 inch cast iron skillet.
2. Place skillet in the oven and heat oven to 425* F.
3. While oven is heating, mix your batter, combine the following ingredients:

- 1 ½ cups buttermilk flavored cornmeal mix
- ½ cup sugar
- 1 egg
- ¾ cup milk

4. Pour into hot skillet.
5. Bake 425*F for 20-25 minutes

Creel's "Must Have" Traditional Cornbread

This is Barry Creel's recipe for cornbread. It is prepared with unleavened cornmeal and is a good choice for those who are trying to keep a **gluten free** diet. For gluten free versions of any of the breads in the "Cornbread with Stuff in it" section, you can use this cornbread recipe and just add the stuff to it.

Barry is a renowned and serious cook. He has very strong opinions about cornmeal color and texture. So much so, that he has been known to smuggle this very recipe of prepared cornbread north of the Mason-Dixon line rather than risk settling for an unsatisfactory pone. He and I are in complete agreement when we say that cornbread should be served, crust side up, on a plate. (Barry has offered the photograph below demonstrating proper cornbread plating.) You will read more about that when you read about his Granny's Squash Casserole in the side dish section.

Creel's "Must-Have" Traditional Cornbread Recipe

Ingredients

1. 2 cups White Cornmeal
2. 2 teaspoons Baking powder
3. 1 teaspoon Baking Soda
4. 3/4 teaspoon salt
5. 2 eggs, slightly beaten
6. 2 cups Buttermilk
7. 2 Tablespoons Canola oil

Instructions

1. Preheat oven to 450 degrees.
2. Heat cast iron skillet in hot oven for 5-7 minutes before adding Cornbread batter.
3. In a medium sized bowl, mix Cornmeal, baking powder, baking soda, and salt.
4. Add eggs, buttermilk and oil.
5. Stir just until dry ingredients are moistened.
6. Pour into hot skillet.

7. Bake for 25 minutes.
8. Turn out of skillet onto a plate as soon as the Cornbread comes out of the oven.
9. Serve with crust facing up.

Granny Tom's Patted Cornpone

Granny Tom and the Nichols Girls

Like many country girls born in 1903, Tommie Nichols came from a large close-knit family. She was next to the youngest of a fairly large tribe. I didn't know them all, but I did know Daisy, Sudie, Verlia, Hattie Alice, and my Granny Tom.

The Nichols girls were all very talented with a needle, crochet hook, hair clipper, skillet, or gardening tool. They were both dignified and down-to-earth. They absolutely adored one another and loved to spend time together. Even though they all lived in very close proximity to one another, every once in a while they would have a "spend-the-night-party" and all get together just to go to sleep and wake up in the morning together at my Granny Tom's house. Because we lived next door, I got to come to the spend-the-night party and usually be Aunt Sude's bed buddy. As an added treat, they would let me drink coffee at breakfast with lots of milk and sugar.

I loved all of my great-aunts. The Nichols girls were like a live aging version of *Petticoat Junction* to me. Aunt Sude was blonde. She would giggle and grin when she would sit down at the church piano and play Little Brown Jug until she was scolded about her choice of song.

Aunt Verlia was a redhead. She adored her husband and she loved to tell me stories about her romance with Uncle Foster. He died of lung cancer the same year the Surgeon General explained how cigarettes would kill you. That was also the year Papa Jack gave up his unfiltered Camels.

Hattie Alice was the youngest of the Nichols girls. She had jet black hair and she taught me to harmonize and sing alto in the choir. My Mama often calls me "Hattie" because we have so much in common… even though Tommie was my Granny. We both love to create something out of nothing, always trying to learn a new trick, and both of us have brown as our favorite color.

Aunt Daisy was the oldest, and she was an amazement to all that knew her for being a woman ahead of her time. She left her husband and lived on her own merely because she wanted her independence. That was unheard of at the time. She wore pants forty years before women were "allowed" to do such things. She was content living with a collie dog that looked like Lassie. She was also the one that brought about Granny being called "Tom."

It was Aunt Daisy's responsibility to comb Granny's hair when she was a little girl. Granny's name was Dona Ione and little Dona Ione absolutely hated having her long dark blond hair combed. Daisy came up with an easy solution for that. She and Sudie took little Dona Ione and a big pair of scissors out in the woods and cut all of her hair off. When Dona Ione came back out of the woods, their father, a self-taught veterinarian, said "Who is this little boy? His name must be Tom!" She was Tommie for the rest of her 91 years of life.

I adored my great aunts, the Nichols girls, and when my daughter was born, I named her Nicole in honor of all of them. Ironically, Nicole, who was named after all of those girls, is the mother of three boys. I gave her Granny Tom's rocking chair to rock those baby boys in. Granny also gave an easy chair to me that had belonged to Aunt Daisy. One day, I will pass it down to my youngest daughter, Daisy, who is her namesake.

Granny made cornbread different from anyone else I have ever seen. She would make the dough fairly thick and pat it out into two little pones on a cast iron griddle. If you looked, you could see her little hand print on the bread even after it had cooked. Although she made the bread for at least 70 years that I know of, Papa Jack was very conscientious about being available to offer supervision from his rocker at the far end of the kitchen as she made the bread.

Papa Jack loved Granny's cornbread. He would eat it with his meal or he would save it to turn it into a cornbread desert. This was done by taking sorghum molasses or cane syrup and pouring it into a little saucer. A pat of butter would be added to the thick sweet liquid and squashed together with the tines of his fork. Then he would "dance" his cornbread around in the buttery sweetness. He would savor it and eat it slowly, making it last as long as possible.

If any cornbread was left over, he might eat it for supper crumbled up in a glass of either sweet milk or butter milk. Of course, if Aunt Hattie Alice was in attendance, she would eat up that last bit of cornbread, so you didn't really have to worry about what to do with the leftovers. And, as I said before, I am most like her! I can't count the times that I've eaten the last little bit of something as I clear up the serving dishes for dinner. I can hear her beautiful, happy, alto voice saying, "I'll just eat this, Tom, so we don't have to mess up another bowl!" Then "pop!" that last piece of cornbread, or spoonful of peas, few little dumplings, or sliver of pie would disappear behind her smile.

I asked my 1st cousin, Tisha Ione DeShazo-Sydow, if she would come up with a written recipe for Granny's Patted Cornpone. She is Granny's namesake, and is the heir to Granny Tom's cast iron corn pone griddle, so it was only fitting that she contribute the recipe. The recipe and a few of her thoughts are shown below. (She's also got a wonderful recipe of her own in the next section.)

Recreating Granny Tom's Cornpone Recipe

As told by Tisha Ione DeShazo

"Dona Ione "Tommie" Nichols DeShazo's lifetime recipe as best as we can duplicate it.

'This is very close to Granny's, but no one could really make it like she could. This is a chewy whole grain cornbread with crispy crust. NOT fluffy or sweet. "Granny Tom had this at most every meal, except for wonderful biscuits at breakfast. Papa Jack was fond of spreading sorghum or cane syrup on it for dessert, when one of Granny's apple pies was not available.

"Here in Hawaii, they only have sweet fluffy cornbread that is like a slice of cake with a meal. It's horrid to a Southerner & they have no clue about wonderful Southern cornbread.

'Granny's recipe is even different from most Southern recipes, as it's crispier & thinner. My 1st attempt at this was with Bob's Red Mill Cornmeal Medium Coarse ground, but was too coarse grain. Next attempt was much better, using organic whole grain cornmeal from bulk bins at any health food store. I will research what is available & would work well. Whole Foods or Organic Harvest have this in their bulk bins".

First attempt at Granny Tom's Cornpone with Bob's Red Mill Medium Coarse ground cornmeal: too coarse, but very tasty.

Second attempt with bulk organic grain cornmeal: pretty close and tastes just like Granny's. Please note hand-print. This is a standard Granny fanny-pat cornpone characteristic.

"Granny used Cabin Home unbolted (meaning good bran & corn germ are not sifted out), but I doubt that's sold any more. If you use cornmeal mix or processed cornmeal, you completely miss the mark of what this is supposed to be."

Granny Tom's Patted Cornpone

Ingredients

1. 1 ¼ c. whole grain cornmeal (Not cornmeal mix nor processed cornmeal)
2. 1 tsp. baking soda
3. ½ tsp. salt
4. ¾ cup whole milk buttermilk (or plain yogurt + 2 T. water)
5. 2 T. oil
6. 1 T. butter

Instructions

1. Heat oven to 400*F
2. In bowl, mix cornmeal, soda, salt.
3. Pour buttermilk into measuring cup.
4. Heat oil & butter in skillet on stovetop. (9-inch cast iron griddle works best)
5. Pour ½ of melted oil/butter into buttermilk.
6. Stir buttermilk into cornmeal.
7. Mix very well.
8. Let sit a few minutes.
9. Scoop ½ of this & make oblong mound in hand.
10. Turn mound onto one side of heated skillet & press into ½ moon shape.
11. Repeat with other ½ on other side. (*This should result in the appearance of 2 cheeks with a crack down the middle or a circle with a line bisecting it, according to your level of humor*).
12. Bake for 20 minutes or until golden brown and tests done with a clean toothpick.

Notes

CORNBREAD WITH STUFF IN IT

I deliberated over what to call this section that would mean what the title says and sound cute. Fancy Cornbread, High Octane Cornbread, Best Dressed Cornbread, and Sunday Best Cornbread were all considerations. But I wasn't in a very cute mood so I just reverted to what you see above, because that's what this section is: cornbread with stuff in it. We start with the Granddaddy of them all, Crackling Bread. Then we move on to some other really fun and tasty recipes. When you put a pone, muffin, or stick of this bread on the table, you will see faces light up like Christmas trees!

Jenny's Jalapeno Cornbread

Mammaw's Little Baby Loves Crackling Bread

With grandparents who raised large families during the depression, I grew up with the belief that nothing useful should ever go to waste. Both of my grandmothers were brilliant, creative, resourceful women that knew how to well manage a household on a frugal budget.

They both had smokehouses when I was a little girl, but the days of home-slaughtering hogs had come and gone by the time I was old enough to remember. I'm cool with that. I did have an uncle that still raised and slaughtered his own pork. I witnessed a butchering session once and it was sufficient to satisfy my curiosity on that topic. However, while it was source of some interest to my curious mind, I surely am glad that I don't have to go through all that to get a pound of bacon or some ham hock for my collard greens.

Although the smokehouses had been turned into storage sheds, both of my grandmothers still cooked pork skin… from the good old "waste-not-want-not" days… and rendered that skin down into cracklings. They fried pork skins in a skillet until the fat was all liquefied and the only thing that remained were these tasty little cracklings. The cracklings were used for crackling bread and the grease was saved to flavor vegetables or go in a cast iron skillet to make cornbread or fry any number of things. This grease is commonly known as lard.

Cracklings are definitely not just a southern phenomenon. They actually exist in many cultures. In Latin America, they are called *chiccarones*. Those will actually work quite well in crackling bread if you don't have a soul food section at your local grocer. They are also found in Asia and Europe under various names. There are even cracklings made from poultry skins. I am sure they would work just as well in your crackling bread if you do not include pork in your diet. They are known in Jewish cooking as *gribenes*.

If you can't find cracklings, another viable alternative is to crisply fry and crumble your favorite brand of bacon. It's not quite the same, but still quite tasty and a pretty close second!

All cracklings are not created equal

There are some precautionary measures that need to be taken when dealing with cracklings. Cracklings you buy in the store do vary in quality and hardness. Some are way too chewy like shoe leather, or perhaps football leather may be a better comparison since it actually is a pigskin. Other cracklings I've purchased in the store are more like some sort of porcine pea gravel than anything akin to a food product. The worst crackling risk is a real gross-out. Nothing can ruin your crackling bread experience faster than putting a crackling in your mouth that still has a hair attached to it. Now that's just disgusting.

I said all that to say this: <u>inspect your cracklings folks</u>! If they are a bit rubbery, you might try breaking or cutting them into smaller pieces and soaking in hot water before using them in the cornbread. If they are too hard, definitely soak them in hot water before hand. If you find one with a hair on it, just throw that one away and look through the rest of them very carefully. You may want to scald that batch of cracklings in hot water, too, just to sanitize them one more time.

You can cook your crackling bread using any of the recipes in the preceding section for traditional southern cornbread: really hot grease in a really hot cast iron skillet in a really hot oven. That will make the firm crust that is so appealing on the traditional southern style. My own preference for crackling bread, however, is to bake it in a cake pan so that the texture is not so complicated. The chewy cracklings aren't then competing in a texture war with the crispy/chewy crust. You may want to try it both ways. It's all good!

For crackling bread, I like just a little sweetness and find that adding just a bit of sorghum molasses gives it just the right taste for my palette. If you don't have sorghum molasses readily available, you can substitute brown sugar, or you can just leave it out if you have a seething hatred for sweet cornbread. (I did mention some people have very strong feelings about their cornbread preferences, you may recall.)

Here is my recipe for Crackling Bread, but you can add a ½ to 1 cup of cracklings to any of the recipes in the Breads, Muffins and Sticks section and get a great result. And, just like traditional cornbread, it is up to you to decide if you want a pone, a muffin, a pan or a cornstick. You're one of the grown-ups now, so you get to decide!

Crackling Bread Recipe

Ingredients:

1. 2 cups self-rising cornmeal mix
2. 1 ½ cups buttermilk (if you use buttermilk cornmeal mix, you may use regular milk)
3. 2 eggs

4. 1 Tablespoon vegetable oil
5. 1 Tablespoon sorghum molasses (don't hate me, this is an optional ingredient)
6. ¾ cups pork cracklings (inspected)

Instructions:

1. Preheat oven to 375* F
2. Spray an 8x8 or 9x9 pan with cooking spray
3. Measure all ingredients except cracklings into a mixing bowl and mix thoroughly
4. Fold in cracklings
5. Pour into sprayed pan
6. Bake 25-30 minutes or until lightly browned and center tests done with toothpick
7. Cut into 12 or 16 squares (depending on how hungry everyone is!)

Jalapeno cornbread

I had a good Jalapeno Cornbread recipe in my arsenal, but hoped to include more of my friends' recipes by asking around for their Jalapeno Cornbread recipes. I first asked Tracy McLean, who said, "Yeah, I've got a good Jalapeno cornbread, but there's this other recipe that I really would like for you to look at." That turned out to be her Chunky Muffin recipe, which was unique to her and I really wanted to include. It's later in this section.

I asked my cousin, Tisha, and she said, "Well, I've got Granny Tom's iron griddle and I was thinking about recreating Granny's Patted Corn Pone… plus there is this other recipe I developed when I was living in France with sun dried tomatoes and goat cheese." Of course, I wanted both of those.

I asked my daughter, Nicole, who told me she made her Daddy's Mexican Chili Muffins, rather than proper Jalapeno… which reminded me that I wanted to include those. This is when I also learned she was using Jiffy Mix on occasion for her sweet-cornbread-leaning sweet husband.

I even asked the man that was hooking me up to the lapel microphone at a conference where I was speaking… a complete stranger to me… he said, "If you'd like a cornbread recipe, I'd like to share my recipe for meatloaf that uses cornbread." (You'll find that in the main dish section.)

Then I hit on what I thought was a complete stroke of genius! I would ask my friend, Chris Dantes, a beautiful lady who is originally from the Philippines. She's a great cook and bound to have a great recipe.

"Chris," I said, "If you give me a Jalapeno Cornbread recipe, I can call it Filipino Jalapeno Cornbread!" She laughed and said "I just use Jiffy Mix."

Below is my own recipe for Jalapeno Cornbread, which I did actually bake for Chris Dantes and she said I could truthfully report that it is Filipino-approved Jalapeno Cornbread and she will be using this recipe in the future!

Jalapeno cornbread batter sizzling in the hot skillet.

The cheese will turn brown quickly, so watch your skillet!

Jenny's Jalapeno Cornbread Recipe

Ingredients

1. 1 ½ cup self-rising cornmeal mix
2. 2 eggs
3. 1 can mexicorn
4. ¾ cup buttermilk
5. 1 cup coarsely shredded cheddar cheese
6. ¼ to 1/3 cup jalapeno slices, coarsely chopped (depending on your heat tolerance)

Instructions

1. Put enough oil in an iron skillet to barely run when held sideways.
2. Place skillet in the oven and heat oven to 450*F.
3. While the oven is heating, mix all ingredients with a spoon.
4. Remove heated skillet from the oven and pour batter in hot oil.
5. Bake for 20-25 minutes, until browned on top and toothpick or sharp knife inserted into bread comes out clean.
6. Run a knife around the edges of the bread and then turn onto a plate for serving.

Mexican Chili and Chihuahua Muffins

As mentioned above, Nicole remembers fondly her Daddy making chili and cornbread. Greg Holt's chili recipe was elaborate and ever changing, I can well remember some of his earlier experiments with chocolate, cinnamon, sage, and cayenne pepper. He mastered chili and it was hard not to keep filling your bowl until you were miserably full. Although his chili recipes could be fairly complex, his "Mexican Cornbread" recipe was really simple. Like his chili, it was really good.

Mexican Chili Muffins

I've included it here as two variations. Mexican Chili Muffins are just the original recipe as Greg made it and the Chihuahua Muffins add the complimentary flavor of hotdogs. They are great for a quick lunch or game-day snack that tastes like some sort of Mexican corndog… hence the moniker: Chihuahua Muffins. Serve as you would other corndogs, with ketchup and mustard. My son, Micah Holt, actually calls them "teacup corndogs."

Chihuahua Muffins are a great game-day snack or really fun light lunch (depending on how many you eat!) Serve with mustard and ketchup or salsa.

When I make a batch, I like to do half-and-half, Chili and Chihuahua muffins on a cold-weather weekend day. We eat the Chihuahua Muffins for lunch, then save the chili muffins to have later with a pot of chili. Of course, if you want all of one or the other, just adjust the recipe accordingly.

Inserting the hotdogs is a great chore for any junior cooks you may be working with in the kitchen. My grandson, River, loves putting the Chihuahuas in the muffin tin.

Chili and Chihuahua Muffins

Ingredients

1. 1 cup cornmeal mix
2. ¼ cup finely chopped onion
3. 1 egg
4. ½ cup milk
5. 1 10 oz. can Rotel (tomatoes with green chilies), drained
6. 3 hotdogs cut into four pieces (or 6 hotdogs if you want all Chihuahua Muffins)

Instructions

1. Heat oven to 425* F
2. Spray mini-muffin tin with cooking spray.
3. Combine all ingredients except hotdogs and mix well.
4. Fill each muffin holder about half full.
5. Add hotdogs alternating between holders.
6. Complete filling the muffin holders that do not hold hotdogs.
7. Bake for 20 minutes or until lightly browned and toothpick tests clean.

HB's Broccoli Cornbread

Early in my discussions with Mama about writing a book about cornbread, she told me I would want to include HB's Broccoli Cornbread. HB is a long time friend of my parents through their activities with the Order of the Easter Star, also known as O.E.S. At the time of this writing, HB is serving as the Worthy Patron (sort of a co-President) of their O.E.S. Chapter. Mama often laughs and says OES stands for Over Eating Stars because they love to have pot-luck dinners. At those pot-lucks, HB's Broccoli Cornbread is always a big hit.

HB is also known for his Banana Pudding. He has also adapted his Banana Pudding recipe to make Pineapple Pudding, too. Since he has a following for both the Banana Pudding and the Pineapple Pudding, he will sometimes bring both AND the ever-popular Broccoli Cornbread.

HB's wife, Carole Beddingfield, sent the recipe to me by email with this note:

"This is a really good recipe. My husband, HB, will be 85 in January and is quite a good cook. He retired after 56 years with Ironworkers Local 92 in Birmingham. He is a Marine. He was in the 1st Marine Division, Asiatic Pacific, during World War II. He is a Past Master of Leeds Lodge #446.

"Over the years, he has done a lot of cooking for the Lodge and our own family dinners. We have been married 17 years this November. We have a son and a daughter and four grandchildren. We belong to Leeds First United Methodist Church and HB is also on the Kitchen Crew at the church.

HB says that cooking is his way of relaxing after a hard day."

This recipe is also fully endorsed by my two youngest daughters, Sage and Daisy. I made the recipe to test it for The Cornbread Bible. I overhead their discussion about how I was making cornbread, but Sage saw me putting BROCCOLI in the cornbread. The batter was completely full of it! Daisy immediately began negotiations for only having to eat a tiny sliver of a piece when dinner was served.

Their tune completely changed when it came out of the oven and they saw it with all of the melted cheese on top. It smelled so delicious, too! Those two little girls ate two slices each and now ask for me to fix Broccoli Cornbread. I don't know about you, but any time you have kids asking for broccoli, that's a good indicator that you have a winning recipe!

Broccoli cornbread from sizzling batter in the skillet to hot out of the oven.

HB's Broccoli Cornbread

Ingredients

1. 1 box Jiffy Mix
2. 2 - 2 1/2 cups frozen chopped broccoli
3. 4 eggs, lightly beaten
4. 1/2 cup butter (1 stick), melted
5. 1 1/2 cups grated cheddar cheese
6. 1/2 cup chopped onion

Instructions

1. Heat oven to 400* F
2. Lightly oil a large skillet (I used a 10-inch cast iron) and sprinkle with cornmeal. Heat skillet in 400*F for 5 minutes.
3. While skillet is heating, blend all ingredients in a large mixing bowl.
4. After skillet has heated, remove from oven and pour batter into hot oiled skillet.
5. Bake at 400*F for 20-25 minutes.
6. Turn hot cornbread onto a plate.

Note: The cheese may make some of the crust stick to the pan. If this happens, carefully remove the crust and puzzle-piece it back to the cornbread. The cheese in the cornbread will automatically help to "glue" it back together.

Tracy McLean's Chunky Muffins

Tracy McLean cooks out loud. Her flavors are bold and delicious. She would rather cook for fifty than five and sees the kitchen as an adventure portal. Any time you go to Tracy's house, you are going to be tempted with something fabulous to eat. I asked her if she would be willing to contribute one of her recipes to the Cornbread Bible. She was tickled to do it.

What I didn't know was that her husband, John, actually used to tease her and say that she should write a cookbook entitled "Everything BUT Cornbread." She tells the story far better than I do, so I'm going to give it to you here in Tracy's own words:

"This cornbread recipe has been slowly, and I mean s-l-o-w-l-y developed over much time. When I was a young girl, growing up in the sixties in Northeast Georgia, we were very poor and lots of mouths to feed. The only bread that I ever remember eating was homemade cornbread, hushpuppies, biscuits, and hoecakes....which was just a big ole biscuit in a cast iron skillet cooked on the top of the stove instead of the oven.

"My Nanny Francine used to make cornbread almost every day. In fact, I can't ever remember not having cornbread. Well, as I grew up and moved away, I married young and made cornbread just fine with no recipe whatsoever and it came out perfect every time.

"Then, I got divorced, moved to West Palm Beach, Fl and didn't find much cornbread cooking going on down there. So, as you might guess, I didn't cook it just for one. I would just go to the local Cracker Barrel and get it when I wanted it. I guess you could say I went about 10 years without making any.

"Then, I got re-married and decided that I was going to cook some cornbread for my new "Florida Native" husband, so that I could show him what this Southern girl could do with an iron skillet.

"The first pan I made was more like corn mush. When I took it out of the oven, it sloshed over the sides of the pan and down in to the oven....I guess I got carried away with the buttermilk! I made it again and again and EVERY time I made it, it flopped. I guess you could say I had 'cornbread-block', kinda like 'writer's block.'

"So, as any good Southern girl would do, I bought some Jiffy Mix and it came out perfect. Little did I know, my new husband liked spicy cornbread with more of a salty taste. I am not a quitter, so I made at least 50 pans of different types; some made it, some didn't, until I got it down pat.

"Now, that I have been married over 16 years, my husband says that I make the best cornbread he has ever tasted! My experimentation stage evidently, was not in vain. I now can make about 50 different kinds of cornbread, but this is by far, my favorite and it's kept him pleased for many years.

"This is not for the wimpy, it is very spicy…you can adjust it to your liking. As I was experimenting, I started throwing all kinds of things in it to make it taste good. It seemed as though, the more stuff I put in it, the more we liked it. It was from this experimentation phase that Chunky, Cheesy, Spicy, Buttermilk Cornbread erupted."

Tracy makes these in muffin or stick form and calls them Chunky Muffins for short. Tracy is an accomplished organic gardener. She grows red peppers which she dries and uses in her Chunky Muffins. Tracy uses a self rising unprocessed whole grain cornmeal from Hogdson's Mill. She notes that by using the quarter-inch chunks of butter and cheese, additional butter is completely unnecessary.

Chunky Muffin Recipe
You will need a Large Cast Iron Skillet or Cast Iron Muffin Pan
Oil to grease the pan completely (you can use spray)

Ingredients
1. 2 Cups Self Rising Cornmeal Mix
2. 3 Tbsp Olive Oil (*to keep your Cholesterol down*)
3. 1/2 stick of REAL butter or 4 Tablespoons: cut into 1/4 inch chunks (*to raise your Cholesterol back up*)
4. 1 3/4 cups Buttermilk
5. 1 can of Whole Kernel Corn, drained
6. 1 tsp. crushed red pepper flakes
7. 1 tsp coarsely chopped Jalapeno pepper (*fresh is best*)
8. 1 tsp sugar
9. 2 eggs
10. 1/2 cup extra sharp cheddar cheese chunks cut into 1/4 inch chunks

Instructions
1. Preheat your oven to 375 degrees.
2. Grease your cast iron skillet and place in oven during the mixing and preheating process. The idea is to bring the pan up to the temperature of the oven.
3. Mix all ingredients except the butter and cheese together until smooth.
4. Slowly fold the butter chunks and cheese chunks in at the very end. This way, the cheese and butter will distribute throughout the cornbread and melt in little pockets of each piece.
5. Take your hot skillet out of the oven and immediately pour your mixture in to the pan. If you wait to pour it in, just gently fold it again so that the chunks are evenly distributed. The pan should sizzle a little when you put it in…this makes the bottom golden brown.
6. Bake about 30-45 minutes or until golden brown and you see the cheese bubbling out of the top. If you are making small muffins, the time will decrease.
7. Place pan on a cooling rack for about 10 minutes, slice and enjoy.

Tisha's Fancy French Cornbread

This is the recipe my cousin Tisha Ione DeShazo offered up when I asked if she had a good recipe for Jalapeno Cornbread. The combination of flavors is delicious.

"This cornbread recipe takes ingredients that are symbolic of happy travels in France. It was a time in my life that I had left some very hard, sad events, & illness. Many blessings had replaced this and I met my wonderful husband Steve. (Our dreams & prayers can come true!)

"We traveled with some of his family throughout France & stayed in several castles. One castle owner showed us how to cook some French recipes. It was my first time to taste goat cheese. French women grow their own herbs and use a lot of them in their cooking. I've always done the same since then.

"If you don't have a rosemary bush, plant one & use it often, it lives for years. It's an herb with antioxidants & research shows it helps short-term memory & mental alertness."

French Goat Cheese, Sun-dried Tomato and Rosemary Cornbread

Note from Tisha: whole grain stone-ground cornmeal is not found in all stores. I buy mine from Whole Foods or health food stores with bulk bins or bags of this.

Ingredients

1. 1 1/2 cups whole grain stone-ground cornmeal (Not cornmeal mix nor self-rising)
2. 2 T. plain flour
3. 1 tsp. baking powder
4. 1/2 tsp. baking soda
5. 1/2 tsp. salt
6. 1 cup whole milk buttermilk (or plain yogurt + 2 T. water)
7. 1 egg
8. 3 T. oil, divided
9. 3 T. sun-dried tomatoes packed in olive oil, room temperature
10. Fresh rosemary, remove from stem &rough chop
11. 1/2 cup goat cheese, crumbled

Prep work:

1. Chop rosemary.
2. Add 2 T. oil to a 10" cast iron skillet.
3. Crumble cheese.
4. Drain & chop tomatoes; reserving oil.

Instructions

1. Preheat oven to 400*F.
2. In bowl, mix cornmeal, flour, soda, baking powder, & salt. Make sure no clumps are in baking powder or soda!
3. Pour buttermilk into measuring cup. Beat in 1 T. oil & egg, and set aside.
4. Heat skillet with 2 T. oil, on stovetop over medium heat.
5. Stir buttermilk into cornmeal.
6. Scatter some rosemary into heated skillet. Pour batter over this.
7. Scatter more rosemary and goat cheese over top.
8. Drizzle some sun dried tomato oil over this.
9. Bake on oven's middle rack until golden brown.
10. Put plate over skillet & turn cornbread onto plate.
11. Put knife or spatula on plate under cornbread to prop it up so steam escapes & doesn't soften crispness. Or use cake cooling rack & let cool a couple of minutes on that, then transfer to a plate.

Notes

_____

_____

_____

_____

_____

_____

_____

_____

_____

_____

_____

_____

HUSHPUPPY HEAVEN

You need to know that I absolutely L-O-V-E hushpuppies. They are my absolute favorite form of cornbread. Most people eat hushpuppies as a side-kick for fish. To me, fish is fine and dandy, but it is really just an excuse to eat hushpuppies.

Hushpuppies ready to dip in ketchup and pop into my mouth!

Almost heaven

Living in the southern part of the U.S. gives me ready opportunities for some perfectly acceptable hushpuppies-on-demand through the kind auspices of Captain D's ®. The Captain was my lifeline when I lived in Pittsburgh for four years. Every time I headed home to Alabama for a visit, I would time my trip to get to Morgantown, West Virginia, during the hours Captain D's was open for business. That was the northernmost outpost of sweet tea territory. A large sweet tea, a sack of hushpuppies and several packs of ketchup for the road made that 13-hour drive much more enjoyable!

Just as a side note: If you have never driven through the mountains of West Virginia, put it on your bucket list. New River Gorge Bridge is an absolute world wonder, but even that does not compare to the natural beauty of West Virginia. Now, I must offer a disclaimer here: I cannot state with absolute confidence that my love of West Virginia is not a shade stronger because they fed me hushpuppies and sweet tea as soon as I crossed the state line. As a precautionary measure to insure that you enjoy the experience to its absolute fullest extent, you may also want to eat some hushpuppies and drink sweet tea as you drive across those splendiferous mountains.

The real deal

My earliest recollections of hushpuppies were at church fish fry suppers at Bold Springs Presbyterian Church. Bold Springs was founded by my own family during the early 1800s in a valley near what would one day become Birmingham, Alabama. Imagine the epitome of the little brown church in the wildwood. It is constructed of river rock and sits on a little rise in a grove of dogwoods and giant pines right beside Lake Purdy. No place is so dear to my childhood as that little brown church in the dale.

The menfolk

Everyone had their role for fish fry night. The men would catch and clean the fish. They would have a big vat of oil outside to cook the fish. They would stand around and smoke cigarettes and tell fish stories and jokes and joke each other about their fish stories. They talked and cooked and piled the cornmeal coated bream and perch and crappie high on big platters.

One of the stories I recall was their telling the genesis of hushpuppies. According to the Bold Springs menfolk, whenever men would go off to do some serious hunting and fishing, they would have a fish fry at their camps at night. The fish would be dredged in cornmeal, just the way we cooked them. The hungry men didn't want to share their catch of fish with the dogs, so they would mix some water with the leftover cornmeal and fry that in the grease for the dogs. That would "hush up" the puppies while the men ate their fish.

Now what was never clarified to my satisfaction was how the men ever came to eat the food that had been prepared for the dogs. One must ask: were the dogs more willing to share their hushpuppies than the men were willing to share their fish? I also have to wonder if the poor old dogs got anything at all to eat once the men discovered how great hushpuppies tasted!

The womenfolk

The women would be inside the concrete block fellowship hall arranging the drinks, side dishes and desserts. The drinks would be arranged at the end of the counter to pick up last. No plastic cups, but real glasses of ice would be grouped together. They were mismatched contributions from various members over the years. Some of the glasses would already be filled with sweet tea, ice-water or lemonade. I would usually try to find a Bama jelly glass with the Jetsons or Yogi Bear and get a grown-up to fill it with pink or yellow lemonade.

Sides would usually be right out of the family gardens: green beans, corn on the cob, creamed (we call it fried) corn, fried okra, field peas, mustard or turnip greens, thick sliced tomatoes, green onions, and cucumbers. There would always be devilled eggs, potato salad and cole slaw. Cole slaw was an absolute requirement by the adults, but not really high on my own list when in competition with all the other great food.

The desserts would normally include egg custard that had been baked in little fluted glass cups, delicious pound cake that had at least a pound of butter in it, lightly browned meringue pies with chocolate or lemon filling, and my hands-down favorite: fried pies. The ladies of Bold Springs were absolutely famous for their mastery of the fried pie. Those "in the know" would get a fried pie on their plate first, then fill it with anything else they wanted. No matter what else happened, I definitely wanted to have a fried pie.

Us kids

The kids would be tasked with the transport of "safe" things back and forth. The assignments were probably more to get us out from underfoot, rather than any actual useful purpose we may have served. A glass of tea to one of the men, or another long handle spoon, or a tea towel could be entrusted to us. We ran back and forth between the men and the fish outside and the women and other food inside. It was our primary task to keep everything at the highest possible level of excitement by asking every few minutes when it would be time to eat. The ladies would shoo us away from the food being arranged inside. The men would shoo us away from the hot oil and certain of their jokes and stories outside.

Hushpuppy time

While a fried pie was my favorite dessert, my favorite sound at Bold Springs Fish Fries was when the men outside would tell us to run inside to the women to announce: "It's time for the hushpuppies!" One of the ladies would appear and bring out a great big bowl of hushpuppy batter. We kids would be jumping around in a frenzy of anticipation and get barked a bit more by the adults to stay back from the hot popping oil.

One of the men would hold the big bowl and another would use a big spoon to get just the right amount of the stiff hushpuppy batter on the spoon. The size would normally be somewhere around the size of a small hen egg, but they were not always quite uniform in size. The spoon with the batter would be lowered down close to the oil and carefully dropped into the grease. Steam would rise and the oil would bubble and sizzle and pop all around the hushpuppies. Then as soon as they turned to the absolute perfect color of golden brown, one of the ladies would appear with a platter covered in paper napkins to collect the hushpuppies. One of the men would start scooping out the hushpuppies and laying them on the platter being held by one of the women. Then the next round of hushpuppies would start being fried… but I don't think I ever got to see the repeated process because I was far too busy following that first platter of scalding hot hushpuppies back into the fellowship hall!

Life was grand. A plate of hushpuppies, fresh green beans, field peas, potato salad, a devilled egg and a fried pie and I was a happy little girl in hushpuppy heaven! Sometimes, I would even have a little curled up piece of tender fresh fish that mama had inspected well to be sure I didn't get a bone. Fish or no fish, that didn't matter as long as I had my hushpuppies!

Hushpuppy construction in progress using Granny Tom's old batter bowl.

Basic hushpuppy batter

Ingredients

1. 2 cups self-rising buttermilk cornmeal mix
2. ¾-1 cup finely chopped onion
3. 1 egg
4. ¾ cup milk or water
5. ½ teaspoon black pepper
6. 6-8 cups hot cooking oil (I use a Fry-Daddy knock off)

Instructions

1. Heat your cooking oil to 375*F
2. Mix your batter (all ingredients other than cooking oil), adding milk sparingly just enough to moisten meal and make a thick dough. Batter should easily mound up on spoon to make a hushpuppy ball.
3. When oil is ready, gently drop 3-4 golf-ball sized hushpuppies at a time into hot grease. Do not fry more than 3 or 4 or your oil temperature will drop and turn your hushpuppies into grease-puppies.
4. Fry until a golden brown on all sides.
5. Remove from oil and drain on paper towels.
6. Repeat until all dough has been used.
7. Despite how good they smell, please let them cool enough so that they don't burn your fingers or mouth before you eat one!

Getting jiggy with it

Its super easy to modify hushpuppy batter by substituting ingredients. Here are some things I have tried over the years… you may think of more!

Beer Batter – rather than using milk or water, use beer. It will give your hushpuppies a yeasty flavor.

Green chilies – a small can of green chilies can be added, be sure to lower the amount of liquid to make up for the liquid in the green chilies

Cornfetti – reduce the amount of onions to ½ cup and add a small, single serving can of Mexicorn.

Green onion – Using chopped green onions, tops and all, adds some color to your pups and keeps that nice oniony flavor.

Notes

GRIDDLE CAKES

Okay folks, we've baked it, we've put stuff in it, we've fried it, NOW it's time to cook it on the griddle. I grew up calling this kind of cornbread "Johnny Cakes." It was summertime cornbread when Mama didn't want to heat up the oven. This was in the days before ordinary people had central cooling systems. This form of cornbread is cooked on a griddle or a skillet on top of the stove, much like a pancake.

I've done a little digging, and it appears that these were originally called Journey Cakes. The name later devolved into Johnny cakes (probably by a loving grandmother who made them for a special little boy…. But that's just my imagination.) In some parts of the Old South, they are called "Hot Water Cornbread." They could have been called Lonnie cakes, because my Uncle Lonnie just loved them and he was the one that actually taught me to make them.

I think I like them so much because they are sort of like a modified hushpuppy. They aren't quite as crispy or oily and they are easy to fry up in a super small batch… just one or two… if you want cornbread for one to eat with leftover turnip greens for lunch.

Uncle Lonnie's Johnnies

Ingredients

1. 1 cup self-rising cornmeal mix
2. 1 small egg
3. ¾ cup milk
4. ½ cup finely chopped onion (optional)
5. Ground pepper to taste
6. ¼ cup cooking oil

Instructions

1. Heat cast iron skillet with cooking oil until the oil starts to sheet when tilted.
2. While oil is heating, quickly mix together all other ingredients.
3. Ladle batter, about ¼ cup per cake, into hot oil.
4. When edges are dry and top is starting to show bubbles, flip to brown other side.
5. Cook other side until cooked completely through.

Frances's Mexican Hot Water Cornbread

I asked my friend, Connie Gray, if she had a recipe for Johnny Cakes. "Are you talking about Hot Water Cornbread?" she said. She uses her mother-in-law, Frances's, recipe so that she can cook them "just like mom" for her wonderful fire-fighter husband. I call them "Connie's Johnnies", but Connie calls them:

Frances's Mexican Hot Water Cornbread

Ingredients

1. ¼ cup vegetable oil
2. 1 large egg
3. 1 1/3 cups milk OR 1 ½ cups buttermilk
4. 2 cups Martha White® Self-Rising Enriched White Buttermilk Cornmeal Mix
5. 1 small chopped onion
6. 1 can Mexicorn (corn with chopped red and green peppers)

Instructions

1. Heat cooking oil in cast iron skillet.
2. Mix all other ingredients.
3. Place spoonful of batter in the skillet to fry just enough cakes that there is plenty of room between them and they are not touching.
4. Once the edges are brown, turn once and brown the other side.
5. Remove from oil and drain on paper towels.

Juanny Cakes Benedict for Two

Another iteration of Johnny Cakes was inspired by my son-in-law, Erek, who introduced me to Chorizo sausage. He was also my cooking partner when we won the Fox Bank Chili Cookoff. My other muse on this recipe was Cooper Cannon who said Johnny Cakes with jalapenos should be called Juanny Cakes. Here's an spicy idea for breakfast:

Juanny Cakes Benedict for Two

Ingredients

1. ¼ lb chorizo sausage, fried and crumbled
2. 2 Tablespoons vegetable oil
3. 1 Tablespoon pickled jalapeno peppers, finely chopped
4. 3/4 cup self-rising cornmeal mix

5. 1 egg
6. ¼ cup plus 1 Tablespoon hot water
7. 1 slice onion, chopped fine
8. 3 eggs, scrambled
9. 1 Tablespoon butter
10. Salt and pepper to taste
11. 2 Tablespoons mild salsa
12. 2 Tablespoons shredded cheese (cheddar, Colby or jack)

Instructions

1. In the skillet used to fry chorizo, heat 2 Tablespoons cooking oil.
2. Combine chorizo, peppers, cornmeal, 1 egg, hot water, and chopped onion.
3. Ladle into skillet to make two large griddle cakes.
4. Allow to cook over medium heat.
5. Turn when edges begin to brown to cook other side.
6. After flipping griddle cakes, use second skillet to melt 1 tablespoon butter and cook scrambled eggs.
7. Remove cooked griddle cakes and put one on each plate.
8. Top griddle cakes with scrambled eggs.
9. Sprinkle each with 1 Tablespoon shredded cheese.
10. Pour 1 Tablespoon Salsa over each.

Notes

The Cornbread Bible: A Recipe Storybook

SIDES AND SUCH

Field Peas and Turnip Greens

A hard and fast belief that I hold to with great tenacity is that neither greens (turnip, mustard, collard, what have you) nor field peas (crowders, black eyes, pink eyes, or lady peas) should EVER be put on the table without some sort of cornbread. Cornbread is mandatory. As a matter of fact, anyone should simply be embarrassed to serve either of those essential Southern vegetables 'nekkid' without cornbread of some form or fashion.

Cornbread assisted pea consumption

When it comes to field peas, it's not just that the taste combination is wonderful, it is an efficiency measure. I mean, how do you even get the little rollypollies on your fork if you don't have a piece of cornbread to push them on there with? You NEED cornbread to properly transfer peas from plate to mouth! Don't get me wrong here. I'm not talking about hunkering over your plate with your face three inches from it while scooping food into your mouth with fork in one fist and cornbread in the other… only raising your head to wipe your mouth with your sleeve and take a big loud gulp of sweet tea out of a mason jar.

The proper method for cornbread-assisted pea consumption is quite different from this and quite genteel. As I was taught, you sat at the table with your napkin in your lap. Men were required to wear shirt and forbidden to wear hats at the table. Children were to come to the table with washed hands (and feet if they were particularly dirty from playing outside that day.)

We were always required to sit up straight. We could lean slightly over our plates in order to insure we didn't accidently drip brown pea juice on Mama's pretty print table cloth. The table cloth would usually be white with a pretty fruit or flowers or ribbon pattern print. Nothing even remotely akin to even a partial hunker or slouch was ever allowed. With fork in the right hand and cornbread in the left hand you used them in concert with one another to barricade and roll the peas onto the fork. The cornbread chunk usually soaked up just a little pea juice during the loading procedure.

The proper fork-full was only a partial-load. About half-full was considered a properly loaded fork. A fully loaded fork was courting disaster as a pea avalanche might occur between the plate and your open mouth. The aforementioned properly loaded eating utensil was brought to the mouth to deposit the peas. You then quickly took a little bite of the slightly pea-juice stained cornbread. This was done as one fluid motion so that you could chew them all together.

You did NOT want to load your mouth to where your cheeks bulged out, though. That would make Mama's eyebrows react. They may go up, or go down, or head toward each other. It didn't matter, any eyebrow movement on the maternal parent's part was usually followed by a reprimand from the paternal parent. Just a stern "you better" followed by a "straighten up and fly right" or "quit actin' like you were raised in a barn" or the ever popular "behave your-silly-self" would be delivered without interrupting the general flow of supper table conversation. At that, we had to get a "yessir" out of our mouths as soon as the coast was clear enough for us not to get a second reprimand for talking with our mouths full.

When using the cornbread assisted pea consumption method, it is vitally important to gauge your cornbread consumption so that you don't run out of cornbread before the peas are gone. If you do run out of cornbread, you will then need to get another little chunk. But then you might have cornbread left over and you'll need a few more peas. Surely you can see the vicious cycle you can soon find yourself in. Before you know it, you find you have to loosen your belt and need a post-prandial nap.

One final important piece of advice on this subject: Once you have fully mastered this technique, you will not only be able to gauge the cornbread to pea ratio as an autonomic response, but you will also be able to consume your cornbread in such a way that you get at least a little bit of delicious crust in every bite.

Pot liquor

Turnip greens, collards, mustard greens, or others of that ilk, are consumed by a method quite similar to field peas. But there is a slight variation. While the pea juice is rather incidental to the pea consumption process, the juice of the greens plays a more prominent role. The crust is used to barricade the greens onto the fork, but the midsection of the cornbread is often crumbled right into the juice of the greens. It is then eaten with a fork along with the greens. The juice of the greens is known as *pot liquor*. If there is pot liquor and cornbread left over from a big Sunday lunch, it makes fine light meal for the end of the day. Turnip greens also require pepper sauce, which is made from hot peppers and vinegar. The boiling hot vinegar is poured over the peppers and allowed to steep. After "setting up" for a day or two, the vinegar can be used to season the greens and midsection cornbread crumbles.

Turnip Greens with Cornbread Dumplings

It's always a pleasure to engage in a conversation with my friend, colleague, and fellow Alabamian, Mary Anna Quinn. We usually "get to carrying on" as we discuss growing up in Alabama. While I think her family may have eaten just a little higher on the hog than mine, and we come from different parts of the Heart of Dixie, we have a whole lot of common ground and some really enjoyable and uncommon conversations.

While we are both hard-working career women, we have sat and marveled at how hard our female ancestors had to work. We've related stories of our grandmothers and how they had to work. They had to make the clothes for their families. Wash those same clothes, along with all of the household linens, by hand. The water had to be boiled and poured into washtubs because there were no hot water heaters. They grew their own fruits, vegetables, and meats. Both of us have seen our grandmothers slaughter a rooster as a form of behavioral modification. We have also seen them kill poisonous snakes that might get in the henhouse or slither into the yard.

They cooked in ovens that required kindling and firewood to heat. There was no insulation from the heat of the cast iron stove, which was a blessing in the winter, but a curse in the summer. Not wanting to heat the stove in the summer was the incentive for cooking griddle cakes on hot summer days. They never wasted anything and found inventive ways to "make do" with what was available.

That conversation reminded me of a story that my Aunt Faye told me. Aunt Faye was a professional woman with a career that began in the early fifties, when women often had to choose between family and career. She had to work twice as hard to make half as much as her male counterparts -- without the benefit of a "little woman" at home to take care of the cooking, cleaning, and household chores.

I've always admired Aunt Faye for her intelligence and success and work ethic. She once told me that it must be in our blood, because our Grandma Nichols did hard manual labor all of her life. She remembered going to visit Grandma when she was only about three and Granny Tom was going to show her new baby, George, to her mother. It was always a happy occasion to go down to the old farm.

Grandma Nichols was over 70 at the time and she was on the back porch washing clothes. Of course, in those days, this was hard work which was done with a tub of water and a wash board. Grandma Nichols heard the toddler, Aunt Faye, as she came squealing though the house as fast as she could run to get to her Grandma. Grandma Nichols ran toward her laughing and drying her hands on her apron. She reached out for her precious little granddaughter, and that was the happy act that was her last. She fell before little Faye reached her. She worked up to the last minutes of her life, but she died feeling the joy of the love of her family. Aunt Faye retains that early childhood memory not so much as a tragic event but as a gift because she can recall her Grandma's love and joy.

Mary Anna and I love to share those Alabama family stories with one another. When I told Mary Anna about this storybook, she did a little research into the history of cornbread and its various iterations. She had learned that cornbread had been introduced to the European-descent settlers by the Native Americans. Corn was a Native American staple. One of the three sisters: corn, beans and squash. Cornmeal dumplings were introduced into the pioneers' diet by the Native Americans and they were originally known as Indian boiled cornbread.

Cornmeal dumplings were introduced into my diet by Mary Anna. We were discussing food one day, when she mentioned how much she liked turnip greens with cornbread dumplings. "Cornbread dumplings?" say I with intense interest. This was a new and very exciting concept to my mind. What a perfect combination, to have the cornbread already riding around in the greens soaking up pot liquor! They are just sitting there ready to be scooped right into your mouth with your forkful of greens! How deliciously efficient!

I couldn't wait to test drive them in my own kitchen as soon as she told me about them. We were having company over for supper in just two days, so I went to work. I found fresh turnip AND mustard greens. Two great tastes that taste great together! Then I started perusing the internet to find all of the cornbread dumpling recipes I could locate. After reading about twenty variations on the greens and cornbread dumplings theme, I was ready to try my own hand at it.

Some recipes called for dumplings to live up to their name by just being literally dumped by the spoonful right into the simmering pot liquor. They were then covered and left to take on whatever shape they felt inclined to assume. Others were molded into little walnut-sized balls and placed into the pot liquor. I tried both methods and while both were good, I liked the uniformity and texture of the molded dumplings.

The dough for the dumpling should be slightly stiffer than for hushpuppies.

The dumplings are formed by forming into walnut-sized balls and then rolled in cornstarch.

Place the dumplings on top of the cooking greens in a single layer then gently press them into the pot liquor with the back of a large spoon.

Turnip Greens with Cornmeal Dumplings

Total time for this recipe is about 2 hours, so allow yourself plenty of time.

Ingredients

1. 2 bags frozen turnip greens with turnips
2. 1 cup diced ham (or turkey ham)
3. (additional salt to taste as needed)
4. ¾ c cornmeal mix
5. ¼ c pot liquor (hot liquid from the turnip greens)
6. 1 Tbsp cornstarch for dumplings
7. 1 egg, lightly beaten
8. 2 tablespoons finely chopped onion (optional)
9. Additional cornstarch for dusting board

Instructions

1. Pour greens and ham into a large pot. Mix together and cover with water. Bring to a boil, then lower heat and cook for 90 minutes.
2. After 90 minutes, mix together 1 tablespoon cornstarch and onion (optional) with ¾ cup cornmeal mix. Add egg, then ¼ cup hot pot liquor from the greens to make a stiff dough about the consistency of playdough.
3. Liberally dust a cutting board with corn starch (even if you are a conservative, it's okay this one time. No one will know.)
4. With a dessert spoon (the bigger of the two spoons that comes with a standard five piece tableware set), scoop out a chunk of dough about the size of a walnut or ping-pong ball.
5. Roll the dough in your hands to make it round then roll it on the dusted board and set to the side until all are finished.
6. Repeat until you have used all of the dough.
7. Gently place the dumpling dough balls on top of the greens.
8. Lightly press the dumplings down into the simmering liquid of the greens (pot liquor) with the back of a long-handled spoon.
9. Cover the pot and simmer an additional 30 minutes. **Do not remove the lid while the dumplings are cooking.**

You can serve directly from the pot, or gently remove the dumplings from the pot, pour the greens into a serving bowl or remove to a platter with a slotted spoon. Surround the cooked greens with the dumplings.

The taste and presentation of this dish are wonderful. ***They are even better if you serve with hot pepper sauce.*** While I realize I am veering slightly off course in offering this recipe, it is so simple, so easy and so good! I just had to tell you about it, too. I want you to have the full turnip green and cornmeal dumpling experience!

Robert's Hot Pepper Sauce for Greens

Below is the method we use at the Shambrook house. I taught my Australian husband, Robert, to make pepper sauce and he makes it for the family now. He has entered it into competition in both South Carolina and Tennessee and has won Blue Ribbons and Best of Show for his pepper sauce.

I like the pepper-infused vinegar for my greens. Robert likes to eat the peppers. We are just like Jack Spratt who could eat no fat and his wife who could eat no lean. So between the two of us, we lick the jars quite clean!

NOTE: When working with hot peppers, use gloves if you have them, or wash your hands thoroughly after handling the peppers. Don't touch any part of your body that might be delicate enough to be burned by the pepper juice (mouth, eyes, nose, open cuts, etc.… especially your etc.)

Robert's Hot Pepper Sauce

Ingredients

1. Enough hot peppers to fill whatever cute little bottle or jar you want to use.
2. White distilled or apple cider vinegar – also enough to fill the jar.

Instructions

1. Stab each of the peppers with a sharp knife. This will allow the vinegar to fill the cavity of the pepper and absorb the heat from the seeds.
2. Fill a pretty little container with the hot peppers.
3. Put enough apple cider or white distilled vinegar into a glass mixing cup to fill the container of peppers (remember we are going to be filling the cavities, too.)
4. Heat to a vicious rolling boil in the microwave.
5. Using a funnel, pour the hot vinegar over the peppers. Let settle, shake, to encourage air pockets to rise.
6. Heat more vinegar and fill again.

7. Repeat filling, settling, shaking and refilling until the vinegar level stops dropping (usually about 3 or 4 times, in my experience.)
8. Allow the pepper sauce to ferment, unrefrigerated, for 2-3 days.

Pour the seasoned vinegar on greens, cooked cabbage, or green beans for a little "Southern Twang" to your veggies. It is wonderful! We have a bottle or jar of this on our table at all times.

Aunt Pat's New Potatoes with Cornmeal Butter sauce

Everyone has some sort of superpower. My Aunt Pat has the superpower of being able to feed any number of people on a moment's notice without having anyone scurry out to the store and have everyone leave the table feeling satisfied. She is the modern-day reminder of the parable about Jesus multiplying the loaves and the fishes.

Aunt Pat and Uncle Kyle have done what most people only dream of doing. You know the kind of things people dream of doing… Those things where the sentence begins with: "Wouldn't it be nice if we could just…" [fill in the blank here]. Uncle Kyle retired very early, but even before that, they had all kinds of adventures. The examples would fill this book, but just a few are:

- Buying a large tract of land, and living in the basement with four kids while they built the house over their heads;
- Raising and showing exotic breeds of dogs (prize winners, of course);
- Selling up everything and moving to Florida;
- Selling up everything again and living on a boat;
- Trading the boat for a large 5th wheel RV and living in campgrounds;
- Selling real estate;
- Running a bookkeeping business;
- Marrying in their early teens and maintaining a happy healthy marriage for decades.

I could go on and on, but this should give you the idea. Not only did they do all of these things, they did them successfully. They are entrepreneurs, adventurers, and sweethearts who have faced both heart disease and cancer together with love, faith and optimism. Lucky for me, my parents were best of friends with Uncle Kyle and Aunt Pat, and all of the kids and grandkids got to spend time together almost every weekend at Mama and Daddy's place at the river. The recipe below is one that Mama and Aunt Pat both use for new potatoes. They are both unsure who came up with it, or if they came up with it together. They were forever trying to fill the hungry tummies of a crowd of people with something good to eat. They were both budget cooks. I am not sure if this recipe came about to try to fill us up a little more or to see if it would make something taste a little better. Either way, it is absolutely delicious, simple, easy and makes a bowl of boiled potatoes very special.

This recipe is not only delicious and inexpensive, it reminds me of two of my role models, Mama and Aunt Pat. It reminds me of what great times we all had at the river. Times that were so special for all the generations of our family that my daughter, Nicole, named her first son "River" as a reminder of the love our extended family shared then and now.

Redskin Potatoes with Cornmeal Butter Sauce

1. 4 medium redskin potatoes, washed and cut into large pieces
2. 1/2 stick butter
3. 2 tablespoons self-rising cornmeal
4. 1 teaspoon salt (or to taste)
5. 1/4 teaspoon white pepper (optional)
6. Parsley for garnish (optional)

Instructions

1. Place cut potatoes in a small saucepan.
2. Barely cover with water.
3. Add salt and butter.
4. Bring to a boil over medium high heat.
5. Simmer 15 minutes.

6. Put cornmeal in a cup and add enough of the hot cooking liquid from the potatoes to make a thin batter. (*Aunt Pat says you can use grits instead if that's what you happen to have on hand.*)
7. Pour batter into the potatoes.
8. Allow to cook until potatoes are soft and batter has thickened into a sauce about the consistency of traditional white sauce.
9. Season and garnish with white pepper and/or parsley if desired.

Granny's Squash Casserole

When I say "Granny" here, we're not talking about my Granny, but the Granny of Barry Creel. Barry Creel is a renowned culinary artist who blatantly tempts his friends with irresistible foods that are prepared and presented with nothing less than perfection.

When I heard about the extents to which Barry went to insure his Granny's Squash Casserole met his exacting standards, I asked him if he would send me both the story and the recipe for my Cornbread Storybook. He kindly sent story, recipes and pictures. Read on and enjoy them all!

Creel's Carpetbag Cornpone Caper

As told by Barry Creel

"Nothing quite beats the excitement and anticipation that precedes taking a big trip! That excitement is even greater when the destination is the home of beloved family members! So it is for me each time I travel from Dallas, Texas to the charming cabin home in Williamsburg, Massachusetts of my beloved cousins Jeannie and Mark Martin.

"Preparation always begins weeks in advance with multiple check-lists, 'Must Remember!' piles of this and that, and the all-important list of shoes to be inventoried and packed. The most recent trip north to visit the cousins beloved required even more preparing, wrapping, check-list making and careful packing than all the journeys before! On this particular trip, friends from California to Maine would be converging on the charming little cabin for several days of laughing, silliness, celebrating, and EATING!!

"My cousin Jeannie Martin has been titled 'World's Greatest Cook' or 'WGC' by her husband Mark. There is great truth to be found in those three descriptive words of Jeannie's title, and anyone who has eaten anything from Jeannie's kitchen is sure to agree! Once a date was set for this gathering of friends at Mark and Jeannie's home, Jeannie decided she would throw a HUGE dinner to introduce their Massachusetts friends to the friends visiting. Having spent much time in Jeannie's kitchen on previous visits and being family besides, Jeannie and I spent much time for weeks in advance conversing on menu selections for the big shindig. It was decided that I would add my "specialties" to the culinary offerings at the event: Pecan pies, Cranberry Salad and Squash Casserole.

"Well, right then and there my check-list grew by several items… The Cranberry Salad and Squash Casserole are treasured, dare I say sacred recipes to me and each require certain 'Must have's.' Thank goodness for advance planning! I would not dream of serving Granny's Cranberry Salad in anything but what I refer to as the 'Scriptural Bowl,' that being the round footed Fostoria bowl inherited from my Granny, Sula Ballard.

"So, the scriptural bowl for holding the Holy Cranberry Salad moved to the top of the check-list…along with extra bubble wrap to guide, guard and protect the sacred Fostoria bowl! Then it hit me…what if the stores in Massachusetts were NOT stocking Raspberry Jell-o for some weird reason?? Next on the list: Raspberry Jell-o! I would be prepared! (I never dreamed that fresh Cranberries would not yet be in season when I arrived, which provided its own dramatic tale, but these are not the Cranberry Chronicles now are they??)

"When Jeannie and I would shop in the supermarkets of western Massachusetts, we often discussed the peril of not finding certain items that are common in grocery stores of the South. Good quality frozen biscuits are on the northern extinct list as are speckled butter beans and our favorite….Butter Peas! I also remember Jeannie mentioning at one point that White Cornmeal was hard to find. The possibility of being without White Cornmeal is not good! Especially since I was planning to make Granny's Squash

Casserole which has Cornbread as a primary ingredient…. No Ma'am! I can't be in need of White Cornmeal once I got to Massachusetts!

Now, with today's restrictions in air travel, one must certainly think ahead with what one packs amongst the essentials and unmentionables! White powder, even if it's cornmeal, is sure to raise a few eyebrows of X-ray observers and luggage inspectors! Preferring not to be detained in lock-up while my White Cornmeal is defiled grain by grain, I thought it best to prepare ahead the cornbread for the Squash Casserole and take it with me.

"Perhaps you are asking, 'Why the big deal over White Cornmeal? Why doesn't he just use any old cornmeal? Why not a Cornbread mix?' ' Why?' you ask? Because it matters. The Cornbread that my Granny made to go in the Squash Casserole was made with White Cornmeal, therefore White Cornmeal will be used for the Cornbread to go in my Squash Casserole. No White Cornmeal…no Squash Casserole…at least not made by my hands. I had as soon be tied naked to the town clock than set a Squash Casserole on the table made with cornbread from yellow cornmeal. It would just be tacky. At least to me… And a Cornbread MIX?!? Lord have MERCY…don't get me started…

"The day before departing on my big trip to Mark and Jeannie's the shoe selections had been whittled down to a mere six pair, shirts were pressed and folded, the sacred Fostoria bowl was bubbled and taped…and the oven was heating to 450 degrees. All the Cornbread ingredients were lined up on the counter, the black cast iron skillet was heating in the oven… Once mixed and ready to pour into the skillet, that tale tell SIZZLE, as Cornbread batter met cast iron let me know that Granny's Squash Casserole would be just perfect for its Massachusetts debut at Jeannie's big party!

"After ample cooling time, the traveling Cornbread was double wrapped in heavy duty tin foil and tucked inside a large Ziploc bag. My large carry-on bag was already packed awaiting its final item: The Cornbread! Nestled atop the sacred bubble wrapped Cranberry Salad bowl sat the Cornbread…these two precious items would be carried onboard the plane with me. I only took a chance with the Raspberry Jell-o (another powder!) by packing it in my checked bag. My Cornbread, like the Fostoria, was a far too precious cargo to be out of reach and left to the mercy of the luggage handlers. The Jell-o was on its own!

"It was a long day of travel from Dallas, Texas to Williamsburg, Massachusetts! From Dallas I flew with the Cornbread and Fostoria bowl to Oklahoma City and then on to Baltimore, Maryland. During my three hour layover in Baltimore, I took a photo of my huge carry-on bag with the traveling pone of Cornbread perched on top. I posted the photo on my Facebook where it wasn't long until friends from all over became amused with me traveling cross country with a pone of Cornbread! Why, what could be more natural than having Cornbread in my carry-on? It was going to be the key ingredient in Granny's Squash Casserole, after all!

"There was however a pensive pause when a friend exclaimed, 'How did you get through security with the Cornbread?? It looks like a bomb!!' A bomb?? I never knew that bombs came in the shape of Cornbread!

"Thankfully, the bomb-shaped Cornbread completed its cross-country journey arriving in Hartford, Connecticut safe and sound! Beloved cousin Jeannie met me at the Hartford airport to whisk me, the sacred bubble wrapped Cranberry Salad bowl and the double tin foiled and ziplocked White Cornmeal Cornbread north to the charming little cabin in Williamsburg, Massachusetts!

"As Jeannie and I were waiting for my checked bag to arrive, Jeannie asked, 'Why didn't you just wait until you got here to make your Cornbread? I've got plenty of White Cornmeal....'

"Now she tells me!!!!"

Cornbread contraband smuggled north of the Mason-Dixon Line in Barry Creel's carpetbag.

Granny's Squash Casserole

Ingredients

1. 4 cups cooked yellow squash
2. 1 stick butter, melted
3. 2 eggs, beaten
4. 1 cup Mayonnaise
5. 1 cup Carnation evaporated milk, maybe a little more
6. 1/2 cup grated cheddar cheese
7. 1/2 cup chopped bell pepper
8. 1/2 cup chopped onion
9. A bit of sugar
10. A sprinkle of salt
11. 2 Tablespoons diced pimento (optional)
12. 4 cups crumbled cornbread *(Make the Cornbread from scratch!* [recommended recipe shown below] *Don't even THINK about using a 'mix'. I can promise you it won't taste 'right' if you use a mix! For this recipe, use only the soft inside part of the cornbread and not the crispy outside crust.)*
13. 1 sleeve of Ritz Crackers, crumbled
14. 2-3 Tablespoons butter, melted
15. 1/4 cup grated cheddar cheese

Instructions

1. Cook squash in boiling water until VERY tender.
2. Drain water off squash.
3. Add stick of butter to hot squash and let sit until butter is melted.
4. In a separate large mixing bowl, combine eggs and next eight ingredients.
5. Mix well.
6. Stir in squash, then cornbread.
7. Mix well, one more time. (If it seems a bit dry, add a little more evaporated milk.)
8. In a separate bowl, mix together crumbled Ritz crackers with melted butter and 1/4 cup grated cheese.
9. Bake at 350 degrees for 30-40 minutes or until set.
10. Remove from oven, cover with Ritz cracker mixture and return to oven for 5 minutes.

Cornbread Recipe for Casserole-Worthy Cornbread Crumbs

Ingredients

1. 2 cups White Cornmeal
2. 2 teaspoons Baking powder
3. 1 teaspoon Baking Soda
4. 3/4 teaspoon salt
5. 2 eggs, slightly beaten
6. 2 cups Buttermilk
7. 2 Tablespoons Canola oil

Instructions

1. Preheat oven to 450 degrees.
2. Heat cast iron skillet in hot oven for 5-7 minutes before adding Cornbread batter.
3. In a medium sized bowl, mix Cornmeal and next 3 ingredients.
4. Add eggs, buttermilk and oil, stirring just until dry ingredients are moistened.
5. Pour into hot skillet and cook for 25 minutes.
6. Turn out of skillet onto a plate as soon as the Cornbread comes out of the oven.
7. Allow to cool before crumbling for casserole.

Sue Ann's Cornbread Salad

Sue Ann is my first cousin. I was seven when she was born. I was fascinated by little baby Sue Ann. She was a living addition to my baby dolls and I absolutely adored her. I was just enough older than her that when I was a teenager, she was fascinated by teenaged cousin Jenny. We still have a very special love for each other and we both shared a very special love and admiration for our Mammaw.

I stayed at home for a couple of years when my second child, Nicole, was born. Sue Ann's son, Joey, was just a year older than Nicole. Micah, my firstborn, was in early elementary school years. We were both living on very tight budgets as young mothers and did various things to supplement the family income. She sold Tupperware and I sold Stanley Home Products. One year, we dressed up like Easter Bunnies and delivered Easter Baskets to kids.

I sang at her wedding to her wonderful husband David. She was the wedding coordinator for my daughter, Nicole's wedding. We have been there for each other for the happy times of life and those times that were very difficult. We've both lived long enough now to have had our share of both. We both have strong faith in God and therefore our worldview is very similar.

One of our many adventures had to do with music. It was during the time that our kids were little that I started writing songs and playing them on a live radio broadcast. Sue Ann would get bookings for me to sing at country church "singings" all around the surrounding counties. It was rare if we ever received any money for this… that's not why we did it. Every once in a while I did find a few dollars snuck in my guitar case for "gas money." We did this just for the love of music and fellowship and spending time with like-minded people. We did often benefit from the food served at those country churches. Homemade caramel cake, crispy fried chicken, chicken and dressing, garden vegetables, turnip greens and cornbread, or a fish fry with hushpuppies might be a fringe benefit of participating at one of the "singings."

Sue Ann and I both share Mammaw's love of having a big crowd of people around and making sure they have plenty to eat. When I told Sue Ann about *The Cornbread Bible* she was an enthusiastic supporter (as she always is for me). She immediately offered to share her Cornbread Salad recipe. I've had a "helping" of this at her house on Thanksgiving as this has become a family tradition for the Robinson family. She tells the story of how this happened below.

Sue Ann's Cornbread Salad (as told by Sue Ann Robinson)

"God brought my husband and I together several years ago after I had been through a difficult time in my life. Ours is a love story that began for him prior to our actual "first date". Matter of fact, nearly 3 years before our first date he knew that I was the one God had for him. I just didn't cooperate very well.

"To seal the deal, he planned an elaborate 'first date'…………..he took me 'spotlighting' for deer in a cornfield!! Now, if you have never been spotlighting in a cornfield, you can't imagine what it does to a girl's heart…….just thinking of it……..well…….makes my heart go 'thump-thump'!! Just FYI, he is an avid hunter.

"Back to the story, this display of true love led me to dinner with his family and they introduced me to Cornbread Salad!! To say the least, after I ate my fill and everyone else's fill, his Aunt Mae determined that I "kinda" liked it!! It has been a staple of our family gatherings ever since.

"I hope you enjoy it as much as I did and still do!!"

Sue Ann's Cornbread Salad

This is a layered dish - two layers of each section. Read through the entire recipe before you start.

Ingredients and preparation instructions

First layer (cornbread crumbles):

Pan of cornbread (make as usual), crumbled up

(Sue Ann's Note: *2 boxes of Jiffy Mix, yellow or white, works great!! If you don't use JiffyMix, add a tablespoon or so of sugar to your usual cornbread recipe.*)

Second layer (vegetable mixture):

1. 1 large tomato, chopped
2. 1/2 cup sweet salad pickles, cubed
3. 1 medium onion, chopped
4. 1 large bell pepper, chopped
5. 1 package of Real Bacon Bits
6. Salt
7. Pepper

Mix all vegetables together.

Third layer (dressing):

1. 1/2 cup sweet pickle juice
2. 1 cup mayonnaise
3. In a separate bowl, vigorously mix dressing together until smooth.

If you need more dressing, use this ratio – 1 part pickle juice to 2 parts mayonaise.

Assembly and serving instructions:

1. Place half of the cornbread crumbles as the bottom layer in a clear glass bowl.
2. Top with half of vegetable mixture as the second layer
3. Cover vegetable mixture with half of the dressing.
4. Repeat the layers as shown above.
5. You may garnish with chopped parsley, chives or scallion tops.
6. Refrigerate before serving.
7. Toss together when serving.

(This looks especially festive in a cut glass bowl!)

DRESSING OR STUFFING

First and foremost, *The Cornbread Bible* could not be complete without a section on Chicken and Dressing (pronounced *"chicka-nen-dressen"* as if all one big compound word). This is the absolute Queen of all Cornbread Concoctions.

Some people call it dressing, some call it stuffing and use it to stuff a bird or have as a side dish. My husband, Robert, who is from Australia, calls it seasoning. I just call it improperly constructed if it uses wheat bread rather than cornbread as the MAIN ingredient. Dressing, stuffing or seasoning, just reminds me of elementary school paste if it is not mostly cornbread with lots of good chunky "fixings."

I have placed this section between the side dishes and the main dishes because it is sort of bi-course-ual. It can be a main dish if you put the meat right in the dressing. I can be a side dish if the meat is cooked separately. If the dressing is used to stuff a bird, and the bird is the main dish, I don't know what it would be considered. How can it be a side if it is actually inside the bird? I guess in that case, it is properly an *inside* rather than a side.

The women in my family cook by their senses. Sight, smell, sound, taste, texture all determine when something is ready to go in the oven, or come off the stove, or needs a little more of this or a pinch of that. We don't usually measure anything. We just add ingredients and adjust by our senses. That is the fact that has been the biggest challenge for me in writing this book. Knowing that, I thought I had better give my Aunt Faye a two day warning that I wanted her to think about how to tell someone else how to make a pan of chicken'n'dressing the way she does. At the end of this section, I've included some notes from both Aunt Faye and my Mama on how to make a good pan of dressing.

My aunt, Dorothy Faye DeShazo, was an airline executive when women didn't have jobs like that. Although she lived all over the U.S. and travelled all over the world, she was able to be home very frequently through her airline perks. She lost her southern accent somewhere along the decades of living outside of sweet tea territory, but she never lost her ability to cook delicious southern style cuisine.

Aunt Faye's dressing is my daughter, Nicole's, favorite. Aunt Faye learned from Granny Tom and Granny Tom learned from Grandma Nichols and that story goes on all the way back to the time of the flood. (I'm talking about Noah, not just when they built the dam to create Lake Purdy and the government seized our ancestral lands by right of eminent domain.) We have family recipes that are named after family members that are buried down at Bold Springs Cemetery that were born before the Civil War. But even still, each one of us has our own variations on the theme. Later in this section, I am going to show you how to make your own variation on the theme.

Traditional, old-timey Southern style chicken and dressing often included crumbled up left-over biscuits added to the cornbread. The "pop biscuits" in a tube won't get you there. It has to be biscuits that will crumble. You can use those, bread crumbs, stuffing mix, torn pieces of "loaf bread" or whatever you have on hand, as an extender for your cornbread. My great-grandmother used biscuits, my grandmother used biscuits when my mama was a little girl, but in later years changed to "light bread." My mother and Aunt Faye have now moved from "light bread" to Pepperidge Farms stuffing mix to add to their cornbread.

I'm still old school and just like plain old cornbread in mine. But you had better believe I won't turn my nose up at anyone else's dressing made with cornbread and some other form of bread. I like it, too. But my absolute favorite is 100% cornbread for the bread part. (I do abstain from non-cornbread containing stuffing though, the texture is just too gummy for my taste.)

For moistness, my Aunt Faye uses broth, Mama uses broth and condensed cream of chicken soup. Mama also uses condensed cream of celery soup if she doesn't have celery or feel like chopping. Mama uses milk if she doesn't have as much chicken broth as she needs to make it moist enough. Aunt Beth always uses two cans of condensed soup. They all use eggs. Some folks put eggs in the bread, both raw eggs and chopped boiled eggs in the dressing. Mary Anna Quinn's mom forbade eggs in the dressing because there were already eggs in the cornbread. But guess what, even though they are all different, they are all REALLY GOOD!!!

My grandmothers, great and otherwise, would have gotten both the chicken and the stock from a stewing hen. Hens go through several phases of life. Once they graduate from the egg, they start their career as chicks. Then they scratch their way up to young pullets. Pullet sounds like skillet… and they can end up there if no more laying hens are needed. If they escape the skillet as a pullet, they then go about the business of egg producing laying hens. They are employed in that capacity for about two to three years, generally. After that, they might be kept on as a setting hen to hatch eggs and tend the next generation of young chicks. Unfortunately, those setting positions are very exclusive. It is much more likely that they will be retired as a stewing hen… which is how they get to actively participate in chicken'n'dressing.

Aunt Faye always makes two pans of dressing in order to satisfy the tastes of her divided dressing audience. Some prefer dressing with lots of stuff in it and some prefer dressing without anything in it. I make two or three pans in order to have an extra entrée in reserve. I may make them identical or very different from one another, depending on my tastes of the moment and what I have on hand in the fridge and pantry.

My design here is to help you to make your cornbread dressing to suit your own individual taste and style. You will find that your own recipe will evolve over time by trial and error and whim and audience and ingredients on hand. Rather than dictating a particular recipe to you, I am going to give you an example and then the basic building blocks so that you can create your own dressing (or stuffing) recipe. You will choose items from the building block categories and create your own cornbread dressing masterpiece.

Think of this as sort of a "U-Pick dial-a-dressing" method with four basic components.

1. Bread
2. Liquid
3. Fixings
4. Seasoning and leavening

Butter, broth, milk, and/or condensed soups are the liquids that can be combined and added to make it moist. If you want a stuffing, rather than a pan of dressing, you can eliminate the butter and add less liquid because the juice from the poultry will naturally supply broth and fats for moistness and flavor.

Dressing is boring without what I call "fixings." These could include vegetables, fruits, nuts, berries, or meats. Your vegetables, nuts and/or fruits are added to make it tasty, visually appealing, and texturally interesting. Your optional proteins: chicken, turkey, pork, sausage, or oysters, can be added to make it hardy. Protein is what helps to transition your dressing from a side dish to a main dish.

Before we begin, you are going to have to make some very important personal decisions…

Dressing or stuffing? That is the question.

First, decide what you are making: dressing or stuffing. Dressing has its own real estate in its own cooking vessel. Stuffing is stuffed in a bird (doesn't take a genius to figure that out!) and is cooked with the bird.

Stuffing looks picture postcard pretty, until you begin to serve it. Then it can be rather messy. If you want to eat the bird and dressing together, I put meat in the dressing. If I want to present a whole bird, I much prefer to let the bird be the bird with its own pan and platter and let the dressing reside in its own pan on the side. If you want to stuff a bird, rather than add dressing on the side, you just follow the basic recipe principles, but adjust the liquids and fat downward to about three cups.

Side dish or main course?

Second decision: If you are having dressing, is this going to be a side dish or the main course? Will you be adding meat to the dressing, or serving it on the side? Personally, I love having chunks of meat in my dressing. It's just an efficiency measure. It's a great way to use up that leftover turkey, also. Finally, I can make up a big batch of dressing and divide it into separate pans to freeze for a quick entrée when my chicken and dressing craving hits.

Are you freezing?

If you would like to stockpile for the future, freeze some of your chicken'n'dressing. You could cook the dressing in 8x8 foil pans. Allow the dressing to completely cool, cover with foil, then place in a large ziplock bag to freeze. When you get ready to use the dressing, let it thaw completely in the refrigerator (1-2 days). Then bake in the foil pan, still covered with foil in a 350*F oven for 30 minutes, or until the center is hot. Just be sure to write the date on the freezer bag with a Sharpie and use it within 3 months for best flavor and texture.

Chicken and dressing loaves cooling for the freezer.

You can also bake it in loaf pans and run a knife around the edges of the pan as it cools. Turn the partially cooled dressing loaf onto a platter to cool to room temperature. After completely cooling, wrap in plastic wrap and put inside a ziplock freezer bag to freeze. You can let this thaw in the refrigerator and just slice and heat in the microwave. Or put it back in the original pan, cover with foil, reheat for 20-30 minutes in a 325*F oven and pop it on a platter. You can surround the dressing loaf with green beans or broccoli, garnish the top with cranberry sauce or chutney and serve with gravy for a pretty, easy, and tasty mid-week meal.

What a crock!

If you are cooking dressing for a crowd, your crockpot can be your very best friend. Using the guidelines below, prepare your dressing mix. Spray your crockpot vessel with cooking spray. Gently pour the prepared dressing mixture into your crockpot. Do not pack down. Cover and cook on low for 4 hours. Your dressing will be moist and delicious. The crockpot is also handy to use to keep the dressing warm if your feasting guests are serving themselves buffet-style.

My Own Chicken'n'Dressing Recipe

I'm still old school and just like plain old cornbread for the bread in my dressing. As previously mentioned, you can add other types of bread crumbs to the cornbread, but it will be best if it is MOSTLY or ALL cornbread crumbs. My absolute favorite is 100% cornbread for the bread part. You're probably not surprised, since I'm writing a whole book on cornbread.

I like to make my cornbread the day before, but in a pinch, I can make it in the morning to use that afternoon. It just handles and crumbles better if it has cooled and rested for awhile.

To make the cornbread crumbs for dressing, I cook the bread a little differently than I do for regular cornbread. I use a sheet cake pan, do not pre-heat the pan, and cook at a lower temperature. This is because I do not want the thick crust for dressing. We are making this to make crumbs and the thicker crust from hot popping grease in a cast iron skillet doesn't crumble well.

Not creating a crust is especially important for me. Since it wouldn't be used in the dressing, what do you think would then happen to that unused crust??? Well, I would then have a little gluttonous devil sitting on my shoulder shouting… "It would be a shame to waste all that cornbread crust, Miss Jenny Faye. Why don't you just EAT IT ALL! Bwah-ha-ha-haaaa!" So I use the cake pan so that I will be 'led not' into that particular temptation.

Here is how I make my "standard" cornbread dressing. You can mix and match your own ingredients to come up with your own version from the lists you'll see later in this section, but if you want to follow a recipe for your first cornbread dressing test drive, or just claim this as your own, here is a super easy version that I love. It is a main dish recipe with big chunks of cooked pulled chicken. This is a crowd-sized or multi-meal recipe, but the basic ratio is two parts bread to one and a half to two part fixings to one part liquid. Feel free to downsize as needed.

First you will need the cornbread crumbs:

Cornbread for 10 cups of dressing crumbs

Ingredients

1. 3 cups self-rising cornmeal mix
2. 3 cups milk
3. 3 Tablespoons cooking oil
4. 3 eggs

Instructions

1. Preheat oven to 375*
2. Grease 9x13 sheet cake pan with cooking spray or oil saturated paper towel.
3. Mix all ingredients together.
4. Pour into the greased 9 x 13 sheet cake pan.
5. Bake for 30-35 minutes in a 375* oven.
6. Allow to cool completely in the pan.
7. Crumble by hand into a large mixing bowl.

Jenny's Old Fashioned Chicken'n'dressing

Yield: Serves 12 to 15 (at least)

Ingredients:

1. 10 cups crumbled cornbread (recipe shown above makes 10 cups)
2. 4-5 cups cooked chicken or turkey (pulled apart)
3. 4-5 cups chopped vegetables (onion, celery and carrots in fairly equal parts)
4. 4 large eggs, lightly beaten
5. 4 cups chicken broth (I cook 3-4 pounds boneless/skinless chicken in crockpot to make both chicken and broth)
6. 2 heaping tablespoons poultry seasoning
7. 1-2 teaspoons salt
8. 1-2 teaspoons black pepper
9. 2 tablespoons Clabber Girl baking powder

Preparation:

1. Heat oven to 350°F.
2. In an extra-large mixing bowl, combine all ingredients except chicken.
3. Gently fold in chicken or turkey.
4. Spread the mixture in a large turkey roasting pan or three 8x8 or loaf pans.
5. Pat down with back of large spoon.
6. Bake for 30 - 40 minutes or until lightly browned.

We prefer the vegetables and pieces of meat to be larger bite-sized chunks.

Constructing Your Own Pan'o'Dressing Masterpiece

Now it's time to get down to business. Using *The Cornbread Bible* U-Pick Dial-a-Dressing method, you will make choices from each of the following categories in order to create your own dressing masterpiece:

Bread Foundation

Please choose <u>any combination</u> of the following to make **10 cups of bread crumbs**

- Crumbled cornbread from your favorite recipe (at least 5 cups)
- Stale bread, torn into small ½ inch pieces
- Stuffing mix (like Pepperidge Farms)
- Bread crumbs
- Cracker crumbs
- Panko (Japanese bread crumbs)
- Biscuits, crumbled

Liquid (5 cups of any combination below)

- Chicken broth
- Turkey broth
- Milk
- Buttermilk
- Eggs
- Creamed corn
- Apple juice
- Plain yogurt
- Condensed cream soups (chicken, mushroom, celery, onion, broccoli)
- Melted butter (you may want to add just a little if you use fat-free chicken broth)

Fixings (8-10 cups of any combination below)

- Chopped onion
- Chopped celery
- Chopped carrots
- Diced sweet peppers
- Chopped broccoli
- Chopped boiled eggs
- Shoe peg corn
- Diced green onions with tops
- Green peas
- Chopped Granny Smith apples
- Dried cranberries
- Golden raisins
- Diced dried apricots
- Chopped pecans
- Chopped walnuts
- Cooked, crumbled bulk sausage
- Diced or pulled cooked turkey
- Diced or pulled cooked chicken
- Diced or pulled cooked pork
- Fresh oysters
- Crisply cooked crumbled bacon

Leavening and seasoning (add all of these essential ingredients, but adjust seasonings to taste)

1. 2 heaping Tablespoons of Baking Powder
2. 2 heaping Tablespoons of poultry seasoning
3. 2 teaspoons salt (less if you use condensed soups or salted broth)
4. 2 teaspoons black pepper (less if you want less heat)
5. 2 heaping teaspoons powdered chicken bouillon (more if you did not use chicken broth)

Creating YOUR own signature dressing using *The Cornbread Bible* U-Pick Dial-a-Dressing Method:

Step 1. Select your ingredients

1. Choose 10 cups of bread crumbs (at least 51% cornbread, please)
2. Choose 5 cups of liquid
3. Choose 8-10 cups of "fixings"

Step 2. Assemble your ingredients

1. Assemble bread crumbs, moisture, fixings, leavening and seasonings.
2. Put each ingredient "type" in separate bowls (bread, liquid, fixings, seasonings and leavenings) to insure measurements are correct before you start mixing.
3. Stir together all liquid ingredients. If eggs are included, make sure those are well incorporated into the liquid mixture.

Step 3. Mix your ingredients

1. Sprinkle leavening and seasonings over bread crumb mixture.
2. Stir to combine all dry ingredients.
3. Pour ingredient mixture over seasoned bread crumbs.
4. Mix to thoroughly moisten throughout.
5. Add all "non-meat" fixings. Mix well.
6. Gently fold in meat fixings.

Step 4. Bake

1. Pour into one or more pre-greased baking pans.
2. Pat down into pan(s) with the back of a long handled spoon to smooth top.
3. Bake at 375* oven for 30-40 minutes, or until slightly browned on top and knife inserted in center comes out clean.

Serve with cranberry sauce, chutney and/or gravy.

That's all there is to it. If you are like me, it will be slightly different every time.

Some sage advice from the real experts

As promised, here are some hints, tips, and thoughts from Aunt Faye and Mama. After a two day warning, I called Aunt Faye and asked her to just talk about making dressing and I would type as she talked. She is over 80 years old and still makes a great pan-o-dressing!

Here is what she said:

"First make a round of cornbread. I use a size 12 iron skillet and I just take the self-rising cornmeal mix that you buy in the grocery store and bake it. Sometimes I put an egg in there, sometimes I use buttermilk.

"I buy a package of stuffing mix made from light bread.

"Sometime I use canned chicken broth, but if I'm feeling really smart, I'll buy a chicken and cook it in the pot and use the broth.

"I make the cornbread the day before.

"I season it like Granny did with sage, salt and pepper.

"The chicken broth should be plentiful enough that it will just pour into the pan.

"Depending on who I'm making it for, I put all kinds of stuff in there, usually celery, onions and carrots. I'll separate it and cook it into two different pans so that those that don't like celery or onions or carrots will have some that's plain.

"Some people put in nuts, but if we had nuts, we would eat them up way before Christmas or even Thanksgiving.

"I don't usually put pieces of chicken in there with the dressing. Some people like sausage or oysters, but I just like it as a side dish with the turkey or whatever we're having for dinner.

"I always add a couple of tablespoons of baking powder. It makes it rise nice and not be as tight when you're eating. That way it's not too heavy.

"Cook at 375* or 400* and watch it so it doesn't burn. It has to rise and get clear on the top. Cook it until it has a crust.

"You should <u>always</u> have gravy with it. You can make giblet gravy if you save some of the broth and cook the heart, liver and gizzard with the chicken."

I told Mama about what Aunt Faye had said and she offered some additional tips of her own:

"I always add either cream of chicken or cream of mushroom soup. I also like to add cream of celery soup, sometimes, because it tastes good and it's a lot easier than chopping.

"Granny used to put biscuits in with her cornbread when I was a little girl. We didn't have "loaf bread" except for Daddy to take to work. It wasn't until later on when she changed and started to use bread in her dressing.

"I like to use Pepperidge Farms stuffing mix, now, but I always get the cornbread kind and add it to my big wheel of crumbled up cornbread.

"You can keep a plastic bag in your freezer to keep your leftover cornbread in. That way, you have it the next time you get ready to make dressing. But you know we don't usually have any leftover cornbread, or if we do, I like to crumble it up in a glass of cold buttermilk."

Go forth and make dressing!
So now, you have the basic principles.

You have an example.

You have a customizable method. You have options for ingredients, preparation, presentation, storage, and serving.

You are fully equipped to come up with one or a hundred fantastic, signature dressing recipes that you can call your very own!

Get creative and have fun!

Notes

_____

_____

_____

_____

_____

_____

_____

_____

_____

_____

_____

MAIN DISHES

In this section, you will find recipes that incorporate cornbread into a main-dish recipe. But first, let me tell you how this all started with another story. Get comfortable and sit a spell.

Cowboys, Cronkite and Cornburger Pie

My mother belonged to the Homemaker's Club at Bold Springs Presbyterian Church. This energetic group of ladies did many kind things for the community. They cooked meals for anyone that had a sickness or new baby or death in the family or a new home. They generously swapped recipes. One of those recipes that Mama came by was Cornburger Pie.

Mama was the leader of our church teenage youth group. She would prepare a lesson and a meal for us. The meal had to be good enough to entice the kids to come listen to the lesson. Both were always well-prepared. The first two recipes in this section are from her "Youth Group Collection." Cornburger Pie didn't just go with us to Youth Group, it also became a regular family favorite.

We always ate supper together as a family at the kitchen table. The way the room was arranged, you could see the television while seated at the table. Our supper time would last about an hour.

We usually had the television on. We would typically eat at about the time the local thirty minute news show was getting to Action Sports and The Weather Girl. We tried to be settled in by then because every night a different thirty-minute western would come on. There was Rawhide, with early Clint Eastwood as Rowdy Yates; Maverick, with James Garner (who looks like my Daddy); Sugarfoot (who looks like my Uncle Lloyd). There was also the Rifleman with Chuck Conners playing a single parent named Lucas McCain who was friends with the sheriff, Micah. They were all a part of our supper time. We loved our cowboy shows and after dinner we might watch even more cowboys in one of the hour-long programs like Bonanza, or Wagon Train, or Cheyenne.

Our thirty-minute suppertime cowboys would pretend to shoot each other until it was time for Walter Cronkite to come on and tell us about people really shooting at each other in Southeast Asia. The footage he would show was disturbing. The division in the country about the war was upsetting. The differences between my parents' points of view and my own formative perceptions of the world were very confusing. The CBS Evening News was torture to begin with, but little did I realize it would get even worse!

Suppertime always started on a pleasant note with prayer. We would take turns with who offered the prayer, but it was usually my brother Jeff or me, telling God that we were thankful for the blessing of food sitting before us. Sometimes, if something serious was going on with family or friends, then Mama or Daddy would want to lead the prayer.

Daddy was an electrician during those days. He didn't start his own business until after I was married and out of the house. Our supper conversation would usually include a joke Daddy had heard that day, or a funny story about something his helper had said or done. We would also review the days' events or weekend plans at the river. Report cards, upcoming football games, or extended family news might also be topics of discussion during the commercial breaks from the cowboys.

Parental edicts might also be on the suppertime agenda, which could actually interrupt our regularly scheduled program. Jeff and I were always encouraged to express our own opinions. However, *smart mouth comments* were prohibited. We said "sir" and "ma'am" and were always taught to speak to others with respect. Most often, though, our conversations were light hearted. We were laughing at Daddy's stories or Mama's family news or Brett Maverick's exploits and it was a happy part of the day with family, food and fun.

There were some rare occasions when the conversation would take a more serious tone. The Cornburger Pie recipe made its way onto our weekday supper menu rotation when I was about thirteen. It was about that same period of time, somewhere between the saloons, horses, chuck wagons and Walter telling us "that's the way it is," my parents made a life changing pronouncement. According to them, it was "high time" I started helping Mama with supper. There was no way to appeal the harsh verdict. Daddy made the announcement. Mama nodded her full agreement. There was no call for open discussion of the topic. They were obviously in collusion on this plot to destroy my life.

My time between getting off the school bus and time to start supper was already completely full. I needed to eat my Little Debbie Snack Cake, ride my bicycle, watch I Love Lucy, and play the piano during that time. After supper I needed to watch The Flying Nun or Petticoat Junction or the Brady Bunch on my little 10-inch black and white TV. I also needed to read Nancy Drew or The Hobbit or Mythology and practice singing into my hairbrush in front of my bedroom mirror. How could I squeeze in this oppressive additional responsibility? (Please note no mention of homework. This was done during the 20 minute ride on the school bus so that I didn't have to waste my time on that when I got home.)

It was now my lot in life to start cooking supper two nights a week. What was <u>even worse</u>, on the nights that Mama cooked, I would wash the dishes!!!! Of course, as a normal (slightly spoiled) teenage girl, I thought this was absolute cruelty. I didn't know which I hated worse, dishes or having to listen to Cronkite while I was washing them. It wasn't the actual washing that I minded, it was sticking my hands in dishwater… which was so gross. I'm not sure if Playtex had come out with their gloves by then, but they hadn't made it to Montevallo Road in Leeds, Alabama.

There was also the never-ending struggle to find containers with matching lids for the leftovers, then finding space in the refrigerator. It's no wonder that I ended up doing my Ph.D. in occupational stress! My interest probably stems from the scars of my early adolescence from trying to decide whether the Corningware dish could be crammed into the already full refrigerator or if I needed to find an empty Blue Bonnet or Cool Whip container. Another container that I might eventually have to wash, I might add! This was all added to the incredible strain of trying to wash the dishes without actually putting my delicate hands down into the dishwater.

It is a great mystery and miracle how the kid I was then grew into the kid I am now. I actually find washing dishes satisfying and I thank God my parents forced me to learn to cook. Mama patiently taught me to cook by principle, more than by recipe. That meant that I could be creative and what I cooked was a little different than what Mama cooked. I was surprised to learn that I actually enjoyed cooking and looked forward to the nights when it was my turn to cook (and of course, her turn to wash dishes.) She also taught me to plan a menu and s-t-r-e-t-c-h those food budget dollars. I am so thankful today for those lessons that got me through the leaner times in my life and help me save money while eating great food today.

In the 10th grade, I signed up for Home Economics with Mrs. Harding at Leeds High School. She taught us how to make the best sweet tea in the world. I still use her method. She also added more concepts and recipes to my cooking arsenal, including making yeast breads. I found myself asking people about their recipes. I tried to decipher recipes by taste and texture so that I could reproduce them. Granny, Aunt Hattie, Mammaw, Mama, Tisha, Clovestine Alexander, Nello DeShazo, Mildred Wallace, Bettye Bailey and the rest of ladies of Bold Springs Church influenced my later desire to learn to "put up" food by canning and freezing. And now, here we sit together with my recipe storybook! But it all started with Cowboys, Cronkite and Cornburger Pie.

Notes

Cornburger Pie Recipe

Ingredients

1. 1 lb lean ground beef
2. 1 tsp minced garlic (adjust to taste)
3. 1 Tablespoon Worcestershire sauce
4. 1 can chili beans, drained
5. 1 can black beans, drained
6. 1 can petite diced tomatoes, with juice
7. ½ cup frozen whole kernel corn, drained
8. ½ tsp cumin
9. 1 tsp salt
10. 2 tsp chili powder

Topping ingredients

1. 1 cup buttermilk cornmeal mix
2. ¾ cups milk
3. 1 egg

½ cup shredded cheese may be sprinkled on top after cooking.

Instructions

1. Preheat oven to 425*F.
2. Brown ground beef in skillet, breaking into large crumbles.
3. Add all remaining ingredients and mix well.
4. Pour into lightly greased 2 quart oven-proof casserole.
5. Combine topping ingredients in a small bowl.
6. Spoon topping on top of meat mixture.
7. Bake for 25 minutes at 425*F
8. Remove from oven and sprinkle with shredded cheese.

Beanie-Weenie Casserole

This is another recipe from Mama's "Youth Leader Days." It is really quick, super-easy and will feed a crowd. Cook it in a 9x13 pan. This recipe will easily serve twelve. You can serve this with Cheeto's or Frito's on the side.

Ingredients

1. 3 cans baked beans
2. 1 pound hotdogs, cut into quarter-inch rounds, browned in a skillet with onion
3. ½ cup diced onion
4. 1 teaspoon minced garlic (adjust to taste)
5. 2 Tablespoons prepared mustard
6. Barbecue sauce 1/3 cup
7. 2 T brown sugar

Topping: Mix together with a fork – 1 box Jiffy mix, 1/3 cup milk, and 1 egg

Instructions

1. Preheat oven to 350*F
2. Mix all ingredients except topping in a large mixing bowl.
3. Pour into a 9x13" pan that has been pre-treated with cooking spray
4. Prepare topping mix by combining ingredients.
5. Spread topping evenly over beans.
6. Bake at 350* for 45 minutes

Butterbean Pie

Much of my family still live on the section of land that my great-grandfather bought after they had to move from the Bold Springs Community at the time the Lake Purdy Dam was built. He divided the land among his children. Each generation has subdivided the land a little more. I was fortunate enough to grow up on that family land, completely surrounded by family.

Across the road from my parents and grandparents was the house where my great uncle raised his family. In later years it was inherited by my mother's first cousin Nello. She was a beautiful woman and one of three beautiful sisters. Think of the Andrews sisters. Nello was the blonde. Mariruth had sable black hair and Eloise had mahogany brown. They also had a brother named Sonny who looked like a handsomer version of Humphrey Bogart. He had a career in the Air Force and was a WWII veteran.

All three sisters were talented and creative and loved the finer things of life. They had the gift of transforming simple to elegant with a wave of their graceful hands. Although all three married, none of the sisters had children. They lavished their love and laughter on their extended family and friends. I was a lucky recipient.

Nello was a great cook. My mother and I have both consulted her on some of the heirloom recipes of the family. Nello was well known for bringing bulging folded-tablecloth-covered baskets (yes that's plural) of food whenever there was a potluck gathering. She must have cooked for two days to make all of the food she would bring.

One of her dishes was Butterbean Pie. I think I especially love it because it combines the ingredients of one of my favorite meals: meatloaf, butterbeans, corn and cornbread. Add a green salad and you have a well-balanced hearty meal. Another of the reasons I love this dish is because it reminds me of Nello, Mariruth, Eloise, and Sonny, and that memory makes me smile.

Butterbean Pie

Ingredients:

1. 1 lb extra lean ground beef
2. 1 chopped onion
3. 1 small can tomato sauce
4. 1/2 tsp ground black pepper
5. 1 tsp salt
6. 1 tsp garlic powder
7. 1 tsp Italian herb blend (oregano and basil)
8. 1 can butterbeans or 1 1/2-2 cups leftover cooked dried butterbeans (large limas), drained
9. 1 can petite diced tomatoes, drained
10. 1 can corn, drained
11. 3/4 cup self-rising cornmeal
12. 3/4 cup buttermilk
13. 1 egg

Instructions

1. Heat oven to 375*F.
2. Spray an oven-safe casserole dish with cooking spray.
3. Brown ground beef and onions until meat is cooked and onions are transparent.
4. Add tomato sauce, pepper, salt, garlic powder and Italian herbs to meat and onion mixture. Mix well and pour into casserole.
5. Layer butterbeans, tomatoes and corn.
6. Pour cornmeal into a small mixing bowl. Add egg and buttermilk and mix well.
7. Carefully spoon a thin layer of cornmeal batter to cover entire casserole dish.
8. Place casserole on a cookie sheet or jelly roll pan to catch anything that may bubble out while cooking.
9. Put on center rack in the preheated oven.
10. Cook 20-25 minutes or until bread tests clean with a toothpick.
11. Sprinkle with grated cheese and return to oven for just a few minutes to melt cheese and slightly brown.

Cornbread Meatloaf

As I was in the process of writing this book, I was talking about it to a colleague as I was being "wired up" with a microphone to speak at a conference. The audio technician joined in the conversation and I asked him if he had a good jalapeno cornbread recipe. He told me that he was only moonlighting at the conference and his usual job was working as a cameraman at a network that shot hunting and fishing shows. He said that he his favorite recipe was a great venison meatloaf recipe that used cornbread crumbs. I handed him my card and asked him to email me. He said he would… but the email never came.

I thought it was a great idea, so I adapted my own meatloaf recipe to incorporate cornbread. He was right, it is really good! The texture of the meatloaf is better with the cornbread and ground meat than it is with regular breadcrumbs… at least to my taste. You'll have to try it and see for yourself what you think.

Being a working gal and always trying to conserve energy (both my own and the electric company's), I always make more than one meatloaf when I make them and put one on the table and let one cool for the freezer. Either half or all of the meat can be scooped out and patted into 2-3 tablespoon balls to be baked in pans as meatballs. Those can also be divided for immediate use with some left to cool for the freezer, as well. Choose whatever will work best for you.

I always keep chopped multicolored sweet peppers in my freezer and I like to add those to the meat mixture. They add a nice flavor (assuming you like peppers like we do) and a sprinkling of color throughout the meatloaf.

Cornbread Meatloaf

Ingredients

1. 2 lbs extra lean ground beef (or venison)
2. 1 lb Italian turkey sausage (bulk or removed from casings)
3. 2 eggs, slightly beaten
4. 2 cups crumbled cornbread
5. 1 large chopped onion
6. 1 large chopped sweet pepper (or hot pepper if you are feeling froggy)
7. 1 Tablespoon minced garlic (jarred)
8. 2 Tablespoons Worcestershire sauce
9. 1 teaspoon dried thyme
10. Ketchup, Steak Sauce, or Barbecue Sauce to serve

Instructions

1. Thoroughly mix all ingredients in a large mixing bowl.
2. Divide mixture between two loaf pans sprayed with cooking spray.
3. Cook at 325* for 1 hour.
4. Remove from pans to serving platter drain from any fat.
5. To serve, top with ketchup, steak sauce or barbecue sauce.

To freeze, allow to cool thoroughly. Wrap in foil and place in ziplock freezer bag. Allow to thaw in refrigerator. Reheat in the oven in original pan covered with foil at 350* for 20-30 minutes or until center is warm.

Pot Roast Pie

When we have pot roast with gravy, I love to slice open a piece of hot cornbread and just spoon the gravy right on top of it and eat it with a fork. It is delicious like that. I came up with this recipe as a way to use left-over (or home canned) roast beef that uses the same principle of soaking the cornbread with gravy.

Note: I keep home canned roast beef on my pantry shelf almost all the time, so this is a quick comfort food meal that I can whip up on a weeknight. If you want to learn more about canning beef (on sale) you may want to read my 'I Can Can Beef' article available through Amazon in December, 2012. The article has step-by-step instructions for delicious, tender canned beef and more recipes for using canned beef.

Pot Roast Pie

Ingredients

1. Beef broth
2. 1 ½ - 2 cups cooked roast beef, diced
3. 4- 4 ½ cups diced vegetables (a combination of potatoes, carrots, celery, mushrooms, onions, corn, peas, eggplant, green beans and rutabaga are all good choices. They may be leftover, fresh or a combination.)
4. 2 cups beef broth
5. Salt and black pepper to taste
6. 1 Tablespoon Worcestershire sauce
7. Herbs to taste (whatever you like to use on your roast, parsley, sage, rosemary, thyme, bay leaf)
8. 2 teaspoons minced garlic (about 2 cloves)
9. 4 Tablespoons cornstarch dissolved in 1 cup of warm water
10. Cornbread topping mixture (combine 1 cup self-rising cornmeal mix, 1 egg, and ¾ cup milk)

Instructions

1. Preheat oven to 400*F
2. Mix all ingredients except cornstarch and cornbread topping mixture in a large dutch oven on stovetop. Bring to a boil. Stir in cornstarch dissolved in warm water. Reduce heat and simmer until thickened.
3. Pour into 2 quart greased casserole dish. Gently spoon the cornbread topping mixture in a very thin layer over the top of the beef and vegetable mixture.
4. Bake 30 minutes or until cornbread topping is slightly browned and cooked through.

Corndogs

Our family loves corndogs. We have been known to eat them for breakfast, lunch or dinner. Before I learned to make them, we bought industrial-sized bulk packages of corndogs for the freezer. A little package of six just wasn't safe around our house. A six-pack of dogs was just enough to get a family dispute underway since there are four of us at home and we all firmly hold to the belief that corndogs should always travel to our plates in pairs! Dogs are a pack animal after all, everyone knows that!

The other thing that I wanted to address in developing a "show dog" of the *genus corn*, was to come up with something my gluten-free buddies would be able to enjoy. I haven't tried the pre-fab gluten free cornpups. However, I have it on good authority from my dear friend, Nancy Whitcroft, they are mere mongrel dogs that are not worthy of the corndog title. It hurts my heart to think that Nancy is jonesing for a decent corndog with no adequate relief in sight. So I have swooped in and made it a mercy mission of *The Cornbread Bible* to rectify this horrendous atrocity and come up with a champion breed gluten free cornpup.

Characteristics of a well-bred corndog

First of all, pick your favorite hotdog. My daughter, Sage, loves all beef hotdogs. I try to opt for low-fat versions for the sake of my cholesterol quest. You should pick the frankfurter that most thrills your own taste-buds or meets any other requirements you might have.

Second, I wanted to make the recipe both gluten-free and easy and quick to make. After all, who wants to spend an hour making something that your family is going to gobble down before the sound of the snap ketchup and mustard bottle lids fade.

My dog's bigger than your dog

It doesn't matter whether you use a large bun-length hotdog, a Little Smokey® or a footlong whopper, so long as you can get the dog covered with batter prior to cooking and cover with hot oil when frying the little sucker up.

The hotdogs we use are bun-length and I like to cut them in half because I think they are easier to handle that way AND it tricks my mind into being satisfied with three half-dogs rather than two whole ones. Plus, I think they are super-cute on the little skewers you can easily find in the grocery store.

You don't absolutely *have* to skewer them. You could easily cut the hotdogs into thirds and fry skewerless… or be a total renegade and even fry them whole without skewers. Your choice, it's YOUR dog! There's no leash law on these pups!

For skewers, you can use popsicle sticks, skewers, or even toothpicks if you cut the dog into fourths. The only thing you need to think of is whether the corndog will be too heavy for the stick… or when someone grabs a hot corndog, is there enough of a handle to keep fingers from getting burned. Also, the skewer or stick helps to lower and retrieve the corndog from the oil.

You have to think strategically when working with hot oil.

I use a Fry-Daddy® knockoff cook my corndogs, but you could use a deep skillet or a heavy pan on the stove. The main thing to remember when frying is to be sure your oil is hot, hot, HOT! Around 375*F is where I try to keep it. As you fry, only do a few pups at a time so that your oil doesn't cool down and just soak into your food.

Start heating your oil as step one. By the time you get your dogs ready to dip and fry, your oil will be properly heated. Also, prepare a platter with about a three towel thickness of paper towels to absorb any oil that sticks to your corndogs. If you fry at the proper temperature, there won't be much oil to come off on the paper towels.

Another tip from my Mama here on testing your oil temp: Dip the handle of a wooden spoon into your oil. If it is hot, the oil will bubble around the spoon.

Batter up!

When I told Mama I had developed a great corndog recipe, her first question was: How do you get the batter to stick to the hotdog? That does pose a problem when trying to keep gluten free. Most recipes have flour involved, either in the batter, or for dredging the hotdogs before battering.

The Cornbread Bible Champion Corndog Method (doesn't that sound nice?) includes rolling the hotdogs on a plate of cornstarch before dipping in the batter. It works like a charm and the cornstarch doesn't add a flour-y taste to the corndogs. I once experienced this with a foot-long corndog at a lower caliber fresh corndog stand at the Delta Fair. Of course, I ate it anyway… I think I'd paid about $5 for it and let it never be said that I would waste even an imperfect corndog!

The Cornbread Bible Champion Corndog Method

Dredge (roll around) your hotdogs in cornstarch, then put your skewers in, if you're using them. Pour your batter into a tall glass and sit the glass close to your hot oil cooking vessel. Lower the dog into the glass of batter to coat with batter, then gently lower the corndog into the hot oil. Two to three dogs at a time and two to three minutes at a time will get you there.

After cooking, line them up on a paper towel and start barking at anyone that wants to eat one scalding hot before they've had a chance to cool. If you burn your mouth on the first bite, you can't taste the rest of the dog and that would be such a shame!

The whole process, including swatting away swarming corndog vultures, takes less than half an hour for the best corndogs you've ever put in your mouth!

Cornbread Bible Champion Corndog Recipe

Ingredients

1. 4-6 cups vegetable oil for frying
2. ¼ cup cornstarch for dredging hotdogs
3. 1 16oz package frankfurters
4. ½ cup cornstarch for batter
5. ½ cup cornmeal
6. 1 teaspoon baking powder
7. ¼ teaspoon coarse ground black pepper
8. 2 tablespoons white sugar
9. 1 egg
10. ½ cup milk
11. 16 wooden skewers

Instructions

1. Begin heating oil to 375*F.
2. Line a serving platter with 3-4 thicknesses of paper towels.
3. Sprinkle ¼ cup cornstarch in a plate. Cut each hotdog in half and dredge in cornstarch. Place a skewer in each dredged hotdog half.
4. Mix remaining dry ingredients in a medium bowl. Stir in egg and milk. Pour batter into a tall glass.
5. Dip a skewered hotdog into batter and gently place in hot oil. Cook 2-3 corndogs at a time until golden brown (2-3 minutes). Drain on paper-towel lined platter.
6. Serve with mustard and ketchup.

We enjoy our corndogs with a side of home canned baked beans and sauerkraut.

LAST WORD

Thank you for reading through the recipes and stories. It has been a joy for me to put this together. Consulting with friends and family, collecting recipes, cooking, including my little helpers and taste testers, Sage, Daisy and River, has all been a wonderful experience. The recipes and stories shared by my family and friends have been so much fun for me.

I hope these memories and recipes have helped you to recall some cherished times of your own. You may have noticed there were some cozy little spots tucked throughout the book for you to record a memory or favorite recipe of your own. My intention for these little nooks and crannies was for you to write something in your own hand that you may want to "pass down" to your own loved ones. A favorite recipe for a new member in your family or just any memory you want to share.

If you've found a recipe you like or a story you've enjoyed, please leave some feedback for The Cornbread Bible on Amazon.com.

Thanks for setting with me for a spell.

Blessings to you and those you love,

Jennifer Shambrook

ABOUT THE AUTHOR

Dr. Jennifer Shambrook has a busy full-time job, is raising her second set of children, and enjoys frugal living, food preservation, and maintaining a country pantry in the suburbs of Memphis, Tennessee. Dr. Shambrook is an award-winning author and cook. She has been winning blue ribbons for her home canning projects for over 20 years.

Cooking delicious meals that are super-fast, healthy, low fat and full of flavor is her daily therapy for a stressful job and busy life. She has a Ph.D. in Health Promotion with a focus on stress and how our behavior affects our health. Knowing that her family is feasting on the very best ingredients, with the best taste, and without unpronounceable additives is a measure she employs to lower her stress and increase the good health of her family. Having a well-stocked pantry enables her to skip the fast food places on the way home in order to get a home-cooked dinner on the table in 30 minutes or less.

Made in the USA
Charleston, SC
07 December 2012